C

M000205646

HUGO WILLIAMS
Collected Poems

ff

faber and faber

First published in 2002
by Faber and Faber Limited
3 Queen Square London WC1N 3AU
Published in the United States by Faber and Faber Inc.,
an affiliate of Farrar, Straus and Giroux LLC, New York

This paperback edition first published in 2005

Photoset by Wilmaset Ltd, Wirral
Printed in England by TJ International Ltd, Padstow, Cornwall

A CIP record for this book
is available from the British Library

ISBN 0–571–21691–9

2 4 6 8 10 9 7 5 3 1

Contents

SUGAR DADDY (1970)

SOME SWEET DAY (1975)

SELF-PORTRAIT WITH A SLIDE (1990)

Author's Note

This Collected Poems (which I hope isn't the same thing as a Complete Poems) contains nearly everything I have written to date. It consists of eight previously published books, six of which are currently out of print. Of these last, five were published by Oxford University Press, the other, *Love-Life* (1979), by Whizzard Press/André Deutsch. I have left all of them as near as possible to the original, with only the occasional trim or change of order to some of the earlier books. Here and there I have re-lined a poem, or changed a title for the sake of clarification.

Some of the poems in *Sugar Daddy* (1970) first appeared in pamphlet form from *The Review* in 1969. Some of the poems in *Billy's Rain* (1999) made up the Greville Press pamphlet *Some R&B and Black Pop* (1998). A *Selected Poems* came out from OUP in 1989 and a short selection appeared in *Penguin Modern Poets 11* in 1997.

I would like to thank Neil Rennie for his straight talking over the years. I would also like to thank the editors of the newspapers and magazines who have published my work, especially the *London Magazine, The Review, The New Review,* the *London Review of Books,* and the *Times Literary Supplement.* Without the friendship and advice of Alan Ross and Ian Hamilton, both of whom died last year, everything would have been infinitely worse for me.

SYMPTOMS OF LOSS

(1965)

Still Hot from Filing

The key is still hot from filing, silver
Against skin, like an arrowhead
And sharp. I close my hand over

Its bright surface and feel the fresh-
Cut notches dig into my palm,
Sterile within the wards of flesh,

But purposeful. It leaves its mark
And I become addicted to
The roughness, resolute as bark,

Or wire. I test the hardness of my nail
Against the barbed edge and recognize
A need to understand in Braille

My own antithesis, or that to which
I kneel. Then knowing what it is,
I turn and, keylike, feel an itch

To press my sharpened faculties once more
Upon more malleable stuff,
To watch my influence unlock a door.

Don't Look Down

Don't look down. Once
You look down you own
The fall in your heart,
You rock your stance
On the stone
And hear your ending start.

It climbs up to you
Out of a deep pit
In sentences
Half followed through
And sighs which twist it
Till it wrenches

At your hold, or shows
You as a clown
Whose imitation rage
Will draw from rows
Of seats some laughter, thrown
Like nuts into a cage.

While high in the big top
A white-clad flyer springs
And it is he you were
Who made men stop
And wonder at your wings
So famous in that air,

Until you looked down
And saw your future there
In the dust and light
And suddenly were thrown
Into that pit where
Now you trot each night.

At Six Years Old

At six he thought of death
As some kind of tribute
Paid with a great wreath

To the pure of heart:
Death, rather like a knighthood,
Setting people apart.

Death was courage
And courage death, so that
Even at that tender age

He could contemplate suicide
As a reminder to those
Who laughed when he cried.

For when they saw his closed
Eyes (with any luck
That would be all death closed),

Perhaps they would also see,
As he had done, suddenly,
That his life was his own property.

The Cripple

Holding his hands like strange ivy,
He twines them round his mother's broad shadow.
She is his tree, only with her he grows.
For him she keeps her leaves, her first love,
All the year round, surviving the cold.

Held in her branches like a little kite,
He sees the world below him in the fields,
As somewhere he has long outgrown.

Sometimes he sees a gesture far away,
A bowler flex his arms like wings,

Or someone leaning from a window, like a dove,
Which puts an ache into his shoulder blades
And flight into horizon-smiling eyes.

The Net

Accidents will happen. Swiss
Watches smash themselves
On pavements, rockets miss

The moon and noes and yesses
Get confused in tests,
Answers become guesses,

Till the ministry of friends
Is not so sure it's all
So simple, that it ends

In failure. They must let
You know they want to help
Erect a kind of safety net.

And then the trouble really
Starts: the mesh too gross
For explanations, nearly

Always misses abstract nouns.
Arms fast, legs caught, your words
Go crashing down among the clowns.

The Pick-up

The hardest part is conversation. That is
Providing they both survive
The first shock of assault, the initial
Jolt of finding in a motive

Something more than interest in the bus-
Routes. (A moment when their manner
Falters into a new role.) Both know they walk
Tightropes like duellists and to gore

The enemy is to fall on one's sword.
Both guess at something more, the need
To escape. But the rules allow them
No more help. Now one must take the lead

And the hardest part begins. The same part
Played by the poet, all his senses alive
To the schemes in his head,
The twicking of his thumbs, who yet cannot give

Through a certain reluctance to lie,
To commit himself. A virgin, his first
Words on the page will comprise
Their anxious overtures, carefully nursed

Into something like sanity by similar
Desires: escape and the poem laid neat
In its place. Words having served their course,
The heart goes back to its simple beat.

History

There from the window
Of a car you see her slowly
Turn, a short-haired woman
With a cloak and someone
Touching her. She looks afraid
At something he has said
And turning from him, sees
You watching her and lets
A signal fall between
The two of you, the sudden
Duplication of a sense
Whose reason is most clear.
It is a simple case
Which ends within the radius
Of strangers, almost touching
As they break away. But glancing
Back, they own a sentiment
As yet unformed and lent
An urgency because of it.

Right Moments

The right moment doesn't come
Ticking inevitably round like teatime.

It's not a dental assistant saying:
'Mr Williams were you waiting

For the right moment of the day?
Would you very kindly step this way?'

Right moments haven't got time
To play the waiting game.

They picnic in the rain.
They would do the same again.

And not inside the head.
And not underneath the bed.

But suddenly, without consideration
For the opinion of the population,

Their exacting, clenched desire
Shall be let out into the air.

For right moments don't happen
If wrong ones are never taken.

Right moments are pram covers
For those who have no others.

An Anonymous Affair

We give animals their names as soon
As they are born. It makes them free,
Gives another cut at the umbilical cord.
We do this because we like them to be

People, one to be darker than the other,
Or fleeter. It brings them nearer our world
Of individuals. Sometimes we act almost
As if they were our own tightly furled

Bundles. Names allow them humanity, make us
Blood brothers. But names of people

[9]

Are different and introductions put an end
To hopes of finding simple

Lusting is reciprocal. Our murmured questions
Get no answers till the very end,
When speaking them, we find
That what we half-dreaded has happened.

We have become acquaintances
With nothing in the world to say.
Members of families with relatives in the north.
People. Individuals. Each free to go his way.

The Actor

Sent by his agency to this bright
Box, all his lines straight, knew
Where to die, but was not quite

Sure who he was, or where he'd got
His hat and whether those breathless eyes
Were just his own, each pupil a dot

Of sanity or irony. In the cupboard
His uniforms were headless ghosts:
First, second, third, all safely stored,

Progressing through the acts alone,

Each of them a little more ripped
(Signifying war) than the one before,
The first being left almost undipped

In blood. Tools of his trade, they stand
Representing the passage of time: past
Present and future, ranged close at hand

Upon their hooks, while not far away
Our soldier sits, uncertain of which one
To wear and whether it's all in play.

The Hustler

This man never read books. He'd seen
What they could do to you. They provided
That false sense of security whisky
Gave you, a sense which divided

Your winnings by ten if it
Didn't land you in jail. No. He couldn't live
Without the threat of reality,
The repeated attempts it made to give

His own biography an epilogue. He'd
Shot pool across America since his teens.
He'd been in cabaret before that.
He used to help shift the scenes

After the striptease. They had one set
In the jungle and another in a big cage,
And then he would juggle billiard balls
For those who hadn't gone backstage

To see what was left of the poor fat
Girls for them to enjoy. And after that phase
He knew all about the fronts of girls'
Bodies and also one or two ways

There were of softening them up if you
Hadn't got a dime to your name. In fact
This man never had much time to read books.
He soon found he could have all he lacked

By shooting pool. He used to go to Nero's
Every day to practise, and at night
Learnt how to hustle, which meant knowing
When you were safe and what to do in a tight

Corner if you didn't want both your thumbs
Broken: act as if you owned the whole shop,
Get nice and drunk, cool as ice inside, then
Switch on the talent and watch them hop

Out with their empty money-satchels flapping
Under their coats all the way to the door.
But it wasn't just the dollars that got him.
He'd never been king of anything before.

The way he felt was, anything could be great.
Bricklaying could be great if it built
Up something inside you, made you feel free.
And when he played pool he forgot his guilt,

And why he was there, and remembered instead
That he was Fast Eddie Felson and when
He had a cue in his hands his arms were
Six feet long and he could show any hen-

Pecked, small-time billiard player what
The game was all about. He would slowly fit
The two parts of his cue together, then
Suddenly, *smash* – and afterwards would sit

Back and watch their faces fall as the balls
Journeyed over the felt, directing one another
Into the designed pocket or position. It was
Like watching your destiny. There was no other

Player like Fast Eddie. He was doomed.
It was no surprise to anyone. They all knew
Descent to be harder, feet blindly testing,
Than the upward climb, but only a few

Knew why he kept shooting all night
And all the next day, winning perhaps ten grand,
Only to drink his shots into oblivion
In order not to see it slip away like sand

Towards the evening, remorse arriving
In the morning with the bill. It was a compulsion
Which he had. To win until you lost was
Somehow more rewarding, an emotion

Taken from its simple preliminaries, through
To its natural fate. Not a sacrifice, an act
Like that of love, in which the sensual strokes
Of the game are superseded by the fact.

The Veteran

It is not the scarred face I draw back from,
But the look of reproach I get,
Passing him in the street, the look

Of one alienated from the human race
By the thought of what it has done to him,
Not by what it has done.

[13]

For since he was wounded, fighting,
As he has somehow come to believe,
For his country, he has lived off self-pity

And hate, eyes like bayonets, aimed
Out through the swing doors of the inn,
His fury stretching the silken gauze

Of scar-tissue tight around his lips.
And sometimes, when he is drunk, one has
The story of his life, or the version of it

He has assembled over the years
Now that the truth is buried deep
In some hospital, God knows where. I wish

I could tell him bluntly that nobody notices
His scarred face when he goes resentfully
For his cigarettes: we are all too busy

Fetching our own and anyway we are fully
Conditioned to ugliness, through our surroundings
And in their defence, that nowadays we almost

Welcome it as an old friend to whom
No formalities are owed, tell him that it is
Beauty we cringe from, calling it ugly to preserve

The ugliness we live within, or beauty we try to
Ambush into art, lying in wait for it beside the road
And dragging it to the sheriff, dead or alive.

But I think it would break his heart.

[14]

Driving on the A30

Now I hold exact location
Of my life within a single action.

This, the matched coherence of my route
And eye, the pressure of my foot.

It puts me there beyond the waste
Of nothing ventured, nothing faced.

It keeps me bold and fisted
Like a hawk which ranged and twisted

As we passed, then stooped to wrest
Its victim from a field. The best

In all of us is what we do
When forced to find an answer to

The will which thrusts us forth
In time of urgency, not aftermath.

*

Now it is dark. I only see
The outline of your head is near to me

And pale as headlamps briefly
Press into the gloom then swiftly

Pass. I try to see if you are smiling
And forget to dip. Immediately unsmiling

Drivers flash their hate at me. I glare
Mine back. It makes a fair

Analogy of what we offer in return
For smiles and scowls and how we earn

[15]

Our praise. Now I can see you sleeping
Next to me. A yellow light is falling

On your hands. I try to memorize
The picture as we move, but cannot close your eyes.

Lines on a Train

Too much sailing away. It is always the same.
I say goodbye and I take the ship home.

All night I sit on deck listening to Irish
Songs. Later in the train I see the sun wash

Up the smut of Middlesex. Once back there
Among the familiar signs I feel my presence jar

And a cold hand over my heart. Such partings
Are made easy for us with their reckonings

Of distances and halts, their rival masks
Of gaiety we put on to stop the other's last

Doubts and cut us free. But once the miles
Are set between us, all the sweet guiles

That healed it then are suddenly so close
I see their helplessness. Together we can lose

All thoughts of afterwards, but separate, the irony
Is fast and hard and takes my breath away.

It is all too simple a step backwards
Into the run of things to be considered

Worth the risk. Such moves should not be made
For any clear motive. Good reasons fade

Or turn sour as they win. One should obey
Only the tug on one's heart, the sudden fleeting day

When all the swallows head south without warning,
For it is their own course they are following

And they have no words to reason it away.

Lie

She might have
Been there. That
Was the best
You could say.
That she never
Came was not
What mattered.
It was not
For that
You journeyed
Overland
To get to
Where you knew
She had to wait,
But simply
To check
The image
That she left,

Make sure
She had not done
The same for you.

Fog

Fog has got into this house
Like news of an illness,
Some kind of paralysis.

It is between us and around us,
Like the kindnesses
Of sickroom talk.

We have become visitors
To this house. We keep on
Our coats and stumble against

Familiars of our courtship.

What is it softens us away from
Those days and into this new house
Where everything is indistinct,

Sound-proof, covered with
Green baize? Outside, the fog
Is curling round the sodium lamp

Its sodden fur, and in this house,
Breathing its density between us
With a stench of hospitals.

Symptoms of Loss

It gives off a smell of burning
At first. No definite pointer.
Just a nudge from the sixth sense
And then nothing at all, the way
Instinct yields temporarily to
Reason. The lull before the fray.

The next stage is not so peaceful.
It consists of a furious hunt
In some remote quarter where it is safe
To search without hope: our fears allow
Us there. You'll see we've
Hidden from the truth till now.

This too is the way we react,
How nature postpones the fact for us
Until we are more obedient to loss,
Almost passive. The right places
Then are left until the end,
When the pulse no longer races.

Delphi

Light is present in this valley
    As in no other. It is made of green
And black and comes from the sea.

    There is snow on the cliff face
And in the air, but you can see every leaf
    On the olive trees at the base

Of the mountain and a splinter
   Of rock like a bone on the opposite
Precipice. Light is empty in winter

   And throws back images of distant
Animals and birds which turn and look
   At you from miles away with vacant

Eyes and their wings hardly moving.
   It is part of a stillness
Which is buried in the hillside. Something

   Almost submarine about a silence
Of stones and the ghosts of temples
   And stadiums rising from their immanence.

In Egypt

Turquoise wings on Diamond Harbour Road.
Miss Supra Bhose on Musky Street.
At Karnak, Gouda said 'That will be colossal.'
Cracking sunflower seeds
He told us about his lost master.

Women of the Nile

The women of the Nile wear gold
   Under the black. Bright crescent moons,
Three in each ear and the fold

Of a shawl may hide large axe-
Like diadems, braided gilt. They seek
    To catch about them what the desert lacks

In brilliance of the shining perfect
    Surfaces they shield from the sun's
Cheap metal and the disrespect

    Of men. They cloak their own beauty
In a similar doubt, as if
    Through sight a theft might be

Accomplished, or a kiss. Jewels they must
    Take safely to the grave,
Where ornaments uphold the dust,

    But lips and cheeks they bring
To a husband's bed, who knows
    That a glance is valued like a ring.

Crossing a Desert

    This truck puts an end to dreams,
    How we arrive in great cities
    Simply by wishing on their names:
    Bassora, Isfahan, casting a spell
    On our senses, a coppery bell
    Of their syllables. Or lie awake
    Nostalgic for what might have been,
    Reluctant to invade the wasteland
    When all the leave-taking is over,
    The image out of hand.
    Up here the din is unmistakable: life

Aimed out of the silent shadows
Along its own path, a track into the last
Rays of sun, the meadows of dust.

Some Kisses from *The Kama Sutra*

The Reflection Kiss, one given
Or blown to the reflection
Or shadow of the lover
In a polished mirror
Or on a lighted wall
Or on the surface of water,
Is called the Reflection Kiss

And is but one of many
Varieties of kiss, for example
The Balanced Kiss is a most
Tender expression, for it is placed
Upon a woman's eyelid
Or on a man's fingertips
And is called the Balanced Kiss,

Being neither too strong nor
Too light. Again, the Passion-
Arousing Kiss, that of an amorous
Woman who looks at the face
Of her husband sleeping
And kisses it to show her intention
Or desire is called the Kiss

That Kindles Love or Passion-Arousing
Kiss. And Vatsyayana lays down
Many more varieties of kisses

[22]

Besides those mentioned above
(e.g. the Drinking Kiss), stating
That these will not be needed
By those who are properly in love.

Beginning to Go

I watch your complicated face
In a three-sided looking-glass,

Intent on a radio serial
As you pile the subtle

Darkness of your hair, each morning
Higher on your head. Last evening,

After two bottles of beer
We almost spoke: your sister

Manufactures silk in Bangkok.
She gets about £2 a week

And it's no bloody good. Your own
Work here is harder to explain.

We laugh at almost the same thing,
Uncertain whom the joke is on.

The rift is here already, though we laugh
At it. And though I laugh,

I feel the dried-up sadness
Of it, like age coming into my face.

Miroku Bosatsu

I remember its faint outline
At the back of a museum:
Vague, inviolate, hung

With a fallen radiance
Which seemed to keep from me
Its actual presence.

Even close to, it was an impression
One had, nothing more.

Something fleeting, refracted
By centuries, a mere reflection

Of its true self, as this
Your alien smile, which allows me

No more than a passing guess
At what it really is.

The Hitch Hiker

I have waited days
Beside roads in Queensland,
Got to know their ways.

I am familiar with
their bric-à-brac, pierced
Beer cans, combs, old hats,

Salvage of picnics, breakdowns,
Love affairs, scraps

Of women's weeklies, used perhaps
For sandwiches, or worse.

The *Townsville Times*, September 10,
Carried an item on Floyd Paterson.

What year would that be?
Things seem to last indefinitely
Under the bone-dry dust
Of a thousand travelling salesmen.

Roadsides are desert islands. There
You are cast up like driftwood,
Dependent on the tides and moods
Of motorists, and there you stay,

Flotsam and jetsam of the highway.

Aborigine Sketches

The black men hang their shadows
On ropes underneath the towers.

Their hats slip forward over their eyes
Like the hats of lynched men.

They have been left standing these
Few people, like the dead gum trees,

Grotesquely upright still,
But slowly whitening.

*

The Mission is embalmed in charity.
The dreams of dead

[25]

Misguided German Christians lie an inch
Under the dusty sand that will never
Be sown or broken with laughter.

All day the families of matchstick children
Shift like hour hands round eucalypts.
Hazed in flies, a bleary wolfhound
Shambles across the courtyard – ratbag
Mascot of some disgraced regiment in exile.

*

They hold out to us
Discredited skilled hands they have lost faith in.
We prune them back like jungle for the public good.

This silent Reserve, their country in Arnhem Land,
Is a lopped hand on each of them. Their hands
Are disappearing into the desert and the dreamtime.

*

He is only beautiful
In the manner of his country.
He was burnt by the same enemy,
Was at the same treaty.

And now he lives on a concession
Which shifts with the season,
That he must follow it
As a jackal follows his lion,

Licking at gnawed bones
Till he himself is one,
Hollow and dry as an old tree,
Full of strange, delicate energy.

He can walk a whole month
Into the desert in the dreamtime,
Can scent water on wind
And make rabbits jump into his hand.

He can hit a snake with a stone,
Can play a long, sad note
And burn stories on bark,
Beautiful in the manner of his country.

*

They came to us like lepers
To be cured of nightmares

And we woke them up
And showed them their sores

And hung them like flypapers
In museums called Missions

And said 'We are barely
Keeping them alive', as if

We regretted the way they sometimes
Stirred up their own dust

With a little rum
Bought for them by a tourist.

*

A child sulks upon the lawn,
Exhausted by the lawn's piety.

She wants to take off her dress
And sink into the earth.

For the pink roses have twined
Braceleted arms round her neck

And roots round her body,
Sapping her strength.

Point of Return

I have stared for hours
   At the beautiful maps,
Trying to reduce their powers

   Or scale their significance
To my own. I am
   Familiar with the silence

They return; suggestion
   Of the shifting tides
Beneath the best intention

   To be gone, that boundaries,
Like dying,
   Rouse our fears,

But make us want to cross
   Their lines as well.
It is not flight this

   Instinct, but the will to come
Full circle and return
   With trinkets from the gloom

Of some bazaar, to trespass
   And escape. My fear
Is this, that as

I do, the habit of escaping
Stays with me,
　　Momentum of that breaking

Out, so long ago,
　　Of risking where I stood
For somewhere new,

　　That in the end I treat
Uncertainty as life,
　　Arrival as defeat.

The Stage is Unlit

I come back late at night from your room.
I walk up that steep road
Which looks from the sea like a vertical plank.

My room is cold. The door bangs.
Neither of our rooms has a door which closes.
Mine keeps blowing open. Yours won't shut.

We both have balconies. Yours looks on to a yard,
Mine over roofs to the sea.

I have a better room than yours, but no electricity.
I use old kerosene lamps which smoke and have to be
　　trimmed.

In your room we don't use the light,
For you have a son, not to be woken,
In his blue cot hung with rugs you've made him.

Idol

The sculptor knew it well,
That to locate his god, in wood,
Was to subject its rule.
We know it still,
But sometimes, working on a god,
We are located in hell.

The Waterfront and the Harbour

I give you the open sea to leave me for,
Its many ports and pleasure domes.

You give me a ship, prepared at any time to sail.

But the isles and esplanades of the high seas
Remain unvisited by us,

For we are the waterfront and the harbour,
We meet regardless of shore leave.

The Coalman

The coalman is in the street
And his street-cry is in the houses

Where people are thinking about coal
And their need of it. They think about

The coalman and how his head
Bears all the weight of the coal,

His eyes descending with it into the area
While a lorry creeps along the street.

And they look forward to drawing their curtains
And examining the Amusement Guide

And forgetting the world outside
With all its tiresome two-note warnings

And the coalman going past their doors
With his knowledge of their wretched fires.

The Butcher

The butcher carves veal for two.
The cloudy, frail slices fall over his knife.

His face is hurt by the parting sinews
And he looks up with relief, laying it on the scales.

He is a rosy young man with white eyelashes
Like a bullock. He always serves me now.

I think he knows about my life. How we prefer
To eat in when it's cold. How someone

With a foreign accent can only cook veal.
He writes the price on the grease-proof packet

And hands it to me courteously. His smile
Is the official seal on my marriage.

SUGAR DADDY

(1970)

Brendon Street

I watch the back of the casino: precast walls
Stained black already where
Last year a terrace stood like ours.

In the loading area: ashcans, sports cars,
Scaffolding joints, some mauvish masonry blocks,
A detective paring his nails.

A coiled hose spurts little floods
Of water on the pavement. The brass nozzle
Seems to move away backwards of its own accord.

A van arrives, reversing in a wide curve
To the lift gates where some small gilt chairs
With buttoned seats are waiting.

At seven, the croupiers bristle forth
With cigarettes, handling lighters.
These are the lords of Brendon Street. Their shoulders

Barge against the evening like a ball and chain.
They shoot white cuffs
And kick bright patent leathers this way and that

Among the empties and cats.
A concierge in trousers bows to them
And drags her poodle down the road. A girl I've seen

Looks at my window, but I can't be sure.
I could not move to follow her if I tried.
I stare out through my tent-flaps like a squaw.

Open Window

Voices at night in summer.
I lie in bed
And hear them upside down
And think I am in France.

The Couple Upstairs

Shoes instead of slippers down the stairs,
She ran out with her clothes

And the front door banged and I saw her
Walking crookedly, like naked, to a car.

She was not always with him up there,
And yet they seemed inviolate, like us,
Our loves in sympathy. Her going

Thrills and frightens us. We come awake
And talk excitedly about ourselves, like guests.

King and Queen

They are taming children in the garden flat.
We sit bolt upright as the guardians
Of a tomb. We are kingly with impotence.
Our arms lie along our knees. We might
Be ravelling wool with hollow hands.

Builders

A cage flies up through scaffolding
Like a rocket through time.

Thirty-six floors,
The numbers in white on the windows.

High on the roof I see men clearly
In their yellow helmets, talking.

One of them laughs at something on the river.
A negro turns out his pockets.

Slowly a crane goes by,
Dragging a name through sky.

In a Café

Sometimes the owner's mother
Comes out from the back like a stranger.

She can still take money for things
But keeps it clenched in her fist and has to be helped.

She fills her cup from the canteen,
Lights a cigarette, inhales, you can see

From the way she draws back her lips
That revival withers her.

I almost see it staining her skin
Like vinegar through newsprint on the floor.

Woman in a New House

First morning after our first night here,
Our bedroom full of dusty sunlight,
Whine of a sawmill next door, a radio
In the gardens and the noise of break
From the school in the field.

I am taking things out of old teachests
And packing them away in others. Am I
mad? I can throw them where I like!
My mind is crammed with love and ambition.
The future makes me fall asleep.

The basket I carried the washing in
Was an old wood basket from my father's house.
I found a washing line in the garden
And all my things flapping in the wind
With whip noises. I own the place.

Daybreak

In the morning the birds break up our lovemaking.
They treat us like very young children.
They know it will end in tears.

So without moving
We begin to speak in steadied voices,
Careful as the daylight changes us.

When we look at one another,
We remember we have faces
And use them to be ourselves again.

Sure

Walking upstairs after breakfast
I looked round to see if you were following
And caught sight of you
Turning the corner with a tray
As I closed the bathroom door.

Sugar Daddy

You do not look like me. I'm glad
England failed to colonize
Those black orchid eyes
With blue, the colour of sun-blindness.

Your eyes came straight to you
From your mother's Martinique
Great-grandmother. They look at me
Across this wide Atlantic

With an inborn feeling for my weaknesses.
Like loveletters, your little phoney grins
Come always just too late
To reward my passionate clowning.

I am here to be nice, clap hands, reflect
Your tolerance. I know what I'm for.
When you come home fifteen years from now
Saying you've smashed my car,

I'll feel the same. I'm blood brother,
Sugar-daddy, millionaire to you.
I want to buy you things.

I bought a garish humming top
And climbed into your pen like an ape
And pumped it till it screeched for you,
Hungry for thanks. Your lip

Trembled and you cried, You didn't need
My sinister grenade, something
Pushed out of focus at you, swaying
Violently. You owned it anyway

And the whole world it came from.
It was then I knew
I could only take things from you from now on.

I was the White Hunter,
Bearing cheap mirrors for the Chief.
You saw the giving-look coagulate in my eyes
And panicked for the trees.

Mirrors, Windows

You've discovered mirrors are not like windows
And both are dangerous holes in the walls.

You have to go to them, arms jazzing like a flapper,
And knock your head where a window suddenly
    blurs over,

Or a mirror wilfully bars entrance on itself.
Not knowing which world one cries into, you look at me

And hit the barrier between us, careful
As it reaches out your hand and touches you.

You seem upset by my two appearances, one tangible,
One seen, to your one imprisoned in the screen,

As if that cancelled you. Then turning, you abandon
What you nearly discovered and stagger off, abstracted,

Freed, to an open window where you shout something
At a large dog walking past in the rain.

The Opposition

If I leave the door open she's
Through it in the kitchen. What heaven
As the sugar bag hits the floor

And breaks. Eggs out of the fridge, used
Matches in their place. The scallop shells
She puts in a circle, looking pleased.

Not a moment to lose, our time-study man
Gets out a pressure saucepan and heaves it
Onto a chair where she leaves it.

Turn on a gas jet, eat a banana skin:
Not that she minds being useful,
She just can't wait to be powerful.

Charge

I want to charge down to that water,
Fall over with a bang and stumble
In among the boats and reeds, upsetting

The boatmen and fishermen, swim
Far out in my clothes and pretend to drown.

I am looking after my daughter on this hill.

All the Time in the World

I am in a bathroom.
I hear a car go past downstairs.
I'm putting water on my face.

I hear the car jam still
And my mind comes half awake.

I take hold of the car
And move it back
To when I put water on my face.

And the car goes on
And the water runs away
And again the car jams still.

And when an English voice
Knocks terrified at the door,
I have time to turn off the tap,
I have time to dry my face
– the same face still, but dry –
I have all the time in the world.

Family

In the bosom of the family
A court is in session.

The jury retire.
They run screaming through the streets.

Commuter

1

I was on a train. I missed the station.
Chinese children were looking at my nose.

I looked at them, their faces round as soap,
And saw it hovering mothlike between us.

This was new to me. My nose is breezy,
Even musical, but was never airborn till now.

I smiled uneasily, but the oriental stare
Stopped short of me, focussing on the danger.

Eventually I got out and my nose
Flew swiftly back upon my face.

There was a slight hiss and the train
Disappeared laughing over Asia.

2

Three black mothers in toppling
Starched turbans like mitres laugh
As they copy each other's slow

Needles: orange, grey and pink wool
Tangling all of us in the joke of knitting.

Motorbike

The saddle is frozen solid.
The chronically wet rubber sponge
Inside the leopardskin cover
Crunches like shingle.

I hold my cuff
And wipe off the surface rain,
Lean over and flood the carburettor,
Jump on the start again.

A sneeze.
A little plume of steam.
The old tubes cough up a bit of phlegm
Then fade.

I have chronic catarrh, a raw ankle,
Pinkeye, blackheads and foul hair.
I have a humiliating sheepskin coat
And I lust strangely after a new alternator.

Jab

The disposable hypodermic slips into my biceps.
The doctor looks at me victoriously.

My blood retreats. His smile is threaded to
My gooseflesh, like a hunk of bait.

His pincer thumb converges on two hooked fingers.
Tetanus toxoid flares my fingertips.

The arm is stuffed. It works on a pulley now,
Dangling there like a toy acrobat.

Couple

Sick of me, you search your hair
For the frayed ends
You love to split back to the root.

Your head is bowed.
That hair I would weigh in my hands
Is falling over your eyes.

I don't know what to do
As you pass your time
Perfecting the darkness between us.

Sonny Jim

In my jacket and your jewels
The pusher is always with us.
Our little Sonny Jim.
We can't take our eyes off him.

I came home one night
And he was combing his hair like a mermaid.
I hung my coat on a peg
And it looked to me like a shroud.

Jim smiled lovingly round at me,
Long teeth in a skull. I thought:
'Some secret has dissolved his eyes.'
He bridled yellowly.

Since then we take him everywhere we go.
He is a monkey on a stick.
He only talks about one thing:
Sonny Jim is his own latest trick.

The prettiest boy in his class,
He can tell you all there is
To being a speedfreak at fifteen.
He has the track on his groin.

'They make you roll up your sleeves
And your trousers. I've seen jammed
Forearms come away like plaster
When a bandage is unwound.'

We rock him in our arms
And murmur at the world we bailed him from.
Moses in the bulrushes
Was not more loved than our Sonny Jim.

In the Vacuum

His Carnaby Street frock-coat reminds him of himself.
Flared trousers hold up the dead courtier.

His ghost has sucked him into its vacuum.
He's naked in there, getting smaller.

They're going to garrotte him again.
He's buzzing with horror.

The human honeycomb is trying to replace itself.
The hive is empty. Bees fly out of his ears.

Withdrawal

The spare-part man is breaking up. Only his clothes
Hide the year-old accident
Looming like a becalmed hulk in his eyes.

Reconstituted from memory, he is not an accurate
Model of himself. His weathered skull
Can barely hold on to his hair.

The little faults are wearing holes in his silk skin.
He has had to close down whole areas of pain,
Like disused wings of a childhood.

If he moves at all, the atoms fizz and scream at him
And some burst spluttering over the top.
His life is something from a schoolboy's science kit.

The antidote is too far back for him to know.
He's fossilized, crumbling chalkily in space.
The little bits of him are wild geese.

In Patient

I can find no argument, or even
Dumb insolence to comfort me
In this empty house like an aquarium.
Everything is seen to. They bring me tea

At all the right times, people
From under the stairs with rosy cheeks
And curls, whose steps are so gentle
You never hear them unless a board creaks

Or a door slams. I don't know why,
But after lunch they put a deckchair under a lime
And want me to sit here breathing quietly
Until I hear a bell go in the compound ...

Sailing Wind

All day we fool around the port,
Spending the money like reprieved lifers.
We are as happy as lovers, talking

As if your going ended here
In this blue Ocean Dining Room the last day
Of a month gone on ahead of us.

For a month we have been dying sulkily,
Our bodies futurized, abandoned,
Become symbols of treachery.

Today we are back. The sailing wind
Blows over us.
We tear apart and feel such ecstasy.

Lighter

There's no one in the bar, so the barman
Looks at me and I remember him.

Was it really today
We crowded these sealed windows

Looking for the *Pasteur* in the pink-
Shot waters off Spithead?

The Isle of Wight
Was like a tropic island in America.

Where is it Dad?
There it is.   Boat.   Water.   Fire.

Our table was 'Reserved for Agents'
So you put the sign in your pocket.

Have you got a biscuit sir? Look,
The *QE2* disappearing behind that pier.

I can't see it. Nor can I.
Someone said: look at the ugly ship, darling.

But the *Pasteur* was freshly-painted white
And we were happy as children, staring

Proudly along its solving shape
As the hull drove its name between us.

Gone Away

We leave each other and the habits
Fall away like sight of land.

Now I am featureless
And you are infinite again.

The Elephant Is Overturned

The elephant is overturned
And the snowstorm smashed.

The farm is scattered
And the mini-bricks

Lie old and dazzling
As jewels on the linoleum.

I let things lie.
It seems like donkey's years

Since my family went home.
From where they are

I think they look at me with love
And wonder why my future doesn't take.

Some hand has cut a section
Through this house.

Our bedroom is an open dig
Where we are fossilized,

Naked as the lovers of Pompeii,
Sealed in ecstasy

Three thousand years
Beyond the day we walked in there,

Perhaps passionately, perhaps
For fun. Now we shall never know.

Last Performance

I help you take off your coat
And feel the gesture lock in me.

You look contented with your false lover.
You are genial as a stray dog.

Girl

From the crowded platform
Of this end-of-line resort
You wave goodbye to me.

There are tears in your eyes
As you scan the new arrivals
For your next lover.

Night Club

I watch the ragtime couple
Throw their shoulders in the air,
And you are not here.

'I am in a little saloon
Drinking lemon water
And thinking of many things
And I am sorry ...'

But what's the good of that my love,
If we are strung out like runners,
Losing ground?

I watch the ragtime couple
Throw their arms about each other,
And you are in Germany
Speaking to journalists.

'I remember my mother,
My little daughter ...'

And I remember you. Your body
Furled in dusty Portobello weeds,
Your tragi-comic curls.

Sussex

Broken mauve lightning.
The rooks
Explode upwards
Out of the mauve bracken.

February the 20th Street

A coincidence must be
Part of a whole chain
Whose links are unknown to me.

I feel them round me
Everywhere I go: in queues,
In trains, under bridges,

People, or coincidences, flukes
Of logic which fail
Because of me, because

We move singly through streets,
The last of some sad species,
Pacing the floors of zoos,

Our luck homing forever
Backward through grasses
To the brink of another time.

SOME SWEET DAY

(1975)

The Nestling

Bird who stoops on my sleep,
Lifting me to the ledge
Where your open-mouthed young are waiting,
Tell me what I am.

In the morning I see a body like my own
Dangling from your claws
When I wake, expecting to be fed.

Truce

Each dawn might be winter again –
White empty skies
And all around the block
The curtains white.

Upstairs
We sleep where we are told to sleep.
Without this truce each day
God knows where we would be.

Mercury Flats

Intimate revelations of a stranger!
We look inside his bed
And find a toy engine
With teeth marks.

He took the shaving brush
And put it in the Indian drawer.
He was in the bathroom
With an Indian prince.

Terror struck into his life.
He knew everything.
One day he was walking along.
Suddenly he was back home.

    'Godforsaken part of town, sergeant.
    What are we doing here?'
    'I can't remember, General,
    But I don't agree at all.'

Summer on the Serpentine.
The frogmen shine like seals.
They bark like seals,
Dangling their fins in the water.

Last Night

Wrapped in two dragons with red tongues
You are putting on
Blue eye-shadow for work.
When you get to your feet
Your eyes will be closed again.
You shake some keys or light a cigarette.

I peer into the morning light
But you have disappeared
Into the wings of last night.
Your photograph of Blondin,

Tucked in a mirror,
Hovers between two days.

Money

The tulips press excited faces to the window
Where we are shouting about money.
The banks are closed and we are hungry,
Cut off from our roots like hothouse blooms,
Condemned to holiday
Behind these bars of sunlight
Striping the kitchen where we sit and smoke.
Weakened with too much coffee, we allow
The hours to gather us.
Time is for sale. We toil and spin
To stay on the same spot in the sun,
But money owns the day – unravelling
Our progress like a tapestry.
The tulips shake their heads at us.
Like visitors to a menagerie they come
To shiver slightly at the latest specimen.

Low Tide

Up there
Near the ceiling of our room
Is the high water mark.

Our dreams
Have fallen away from us.
We were almost real.

Dust

I sit bolt upright.
My arms lie along my knees.
The guitar I never use
Stands in a corner by the door.
Its hollow eye
Is the patient, kohl-rimmed stare
Of the Pharaoh's eunuch,
Embalmed with him in Paradise.

Tavistock Square

The Hiroshima silver birch 1963
Is not silver in January.

Mahatma Gandhi looks cold
On his stone shell like a loudspeaker.

They sit down facing him in silence
To talk about their life.

Husband and wife,
Why can't they believe in it?

Century Oaks

The trees are emptying.
The cold young days rush through them
On their way to power.

Down here
We sweep the dead leaves into bonfires
Lest they betray our sympathies.

Empires

When I stare for hours
At the giant purple weeds
Wandering aimlessly over the battlefield
Of this garden, their airborne seeds
Spiralling up over the graves
Of the chrysanthemums
And suddenly decide to clear it all away,
Make it civilized here,
But go on staring at it, hypnotized by the task,
I think my stare
Is Nature looking back at me
With designs on my poetry.

Cherry Blossom
for Soph Behrens

Delicate red flames are finding their way
Out of the dark cherry branches.

[61]

Already they expect the clouds
To reward their fidelity.

Do they come out of the dragon earth,
Or out of my mouth as I had feared?

I see their torches searching my mind
For a clue to their mystery.

They find instead some other little man,
Wandering the hillside with an unknown speech,

Gesturing wildly at the cherry trees.
Are we all the same?

And why are we at war
With easy things we are the reason for?

The cherry-blossom flowers
Wither away from me with a sigh,

As if a great ship were getting under way,
Its coloured streamers

Lifting and breaking finally
As it pulls away from the quay.

I wish the rain could quench this fever,
Which is like an image going on forever.

But rain is not rain to me any more,
It is a warrior at the window pane.

I stand convicted by the laws of nature
Of gazing too long into the future.

O lovely cherry tree, come true.
Together we could celebrate the years.

To His Daughter

A little girl sits on the wall
Colouring something on the other side.
The wind shines her hair as she holds up
A flapping paper to my window.

What is on the paper I don't know.
The hornbeam bends over near her head.
Its two-coloured leaves are like her hair.

Smiling or Hungry

1

The days are circular. My cat sits in them,
Smiling or hungry, like the clock.

For we are all alike,
Even the distrustful Siamese who never purrs.

She slinks down the wall on her belly,
Running some private gauntlet with the sun,
Her ears pinned back.

She it was who devoured all her kittens.

2

The sun creeps towards me across six gardens.
The ginger cats perch here and there
Marking the slothful hours.

I always feel better at this time of day
When the sun falls on the bird table
And the cats are preening themselves on the walls.

Home

A summer breeze
Is drying out the sticky lime tree.
It fills and lifts in the branches
And my ribs heave.

Holidays

We spread our things on the sand
In front of the hotel
And sit for hours on end
Like merchants under parasols
Our thoughts following the steamers
In convoy across the bay
While far away
Our holidays look back at us in surprise
From fishing boats and fairs
Or wherever they were going then
In their seaweed headdresses.

Clouds

They say the clouds are men and women
Fleeing together from the stampede
Their feet slowed down in our dreams.

We saw them for a moment once
And heard their cries
But they slipped back under the hooves
And were lost to the everlasting sky.

The Stampede

Clouds swimming in the paddies.
White peacocks pecking at their own reflections.
Sober as temples, the water buffalo
Are knee-deep in centuries.

From underneath their feet,
From underneath the clouds they are standing in,
A ripple is spreading
Which will muddy the stars.

Expatriates

The vineyard where we live
The one we draw about us on summer nights
Has influenced our poetry
The way it flavours its watermelons with silence.

Pay Day

'At the end of the world,' said the crone
'Are blue and red days
Wrapped and waiting in the shade
And yours for the taking.'

I set one foot on the porch.
The boards creaked. The crone
Looked up from her sleeping with a start.
'The chillis are under the cloth,' she said
'But they ain't been paid for.'

Drifter

People are taking sedatives in boats
Going to America.
Their names drift back to me –
Hollowed out, unpronounceable.
I walk through the crowds in the arcades
And on the sands.

The Water Bearer

When I walk in the streets at night
Following the lamplight to where it falls
Exhausted in my head, some girl
Still carries my love on her shoulders through the crowd
Which sometimes offers up her face to me
Like a book which flickers shut again.

So long I have tried to touch that face
When it drifts for a moment near me on the tide.
So many times I have seen it
Sucked back into the sea
Of all such nights I follow down like stones
To where they lie unfound, unfathomable.

When I wake in the morning, far from her,
This girl, wherever she is sleeping, wakes with me
And takes up the weight of my love for her,
Carrying it back into the world of absences
Where I see her walking alone in the streets
Cursed as she is with being mine.

For her shoulders that are always disappearing
Into the heart of her own searching
Look so calm and beautiful despite it all
That I wait impatiently for the sight of her
Passing again so sweetly through my life
As if she carried water from a well.

First-Night

I pour whisky and ginger ale
Into two glasses.
The world of dew!
Tonight
There is even ice
Laid on by the management.
My leading man
Knocks on the door of my dressing-room

With a box of chocolates.
Congratulations!

Lives

The same train each night
Enters the same station a little late
And different passengers going home
Look up from different books with a start
Their eyes narrowing back into a world
Hardly more shared
As they rake the length of the platform
For something they should find there
The thread of their lives
Difficult to recognize in the gloom.

Lone Star

A child of six who likes the cold wind
Stands in the garden, wondering
What to do now the others are in bed.

From her trapeze
She looks round at another day
Deserting her with promises.

Smudged by the setting sun,
Her cowboy T-shirt is illegible.
She faces into the wind,
Prepared to ride out this last day.

Childhood

Water turns back
From the slow climb north.
Days turn back like children from the dark.

Snow stops falling
On fires, except by the shore.
We are here to see for ourselves
How it covers our footprints with the tracks of deer.

Lullaby

By candlelight one enters Babylon.
Can you hold it still for me?
I want you to shield its light from Syria
The way you would hide your knowledge from a child.
Pick up your feet like this. Don't cry.
The pain will soon pass.
These merchants are my friends.

Now candles encircle Babylon's ends
One candle is enough
To save us from distortion while we pray.
Please, no more school today!
It's tempting to ask
Why roads that lead to Babylon by night
Encircle her so modestly next day.
But all roads lead to blindness at last
For those who are drawn towards their fate.
What you see

Is all that has been left out for you by the night.
The rest will have to wait.

Now word has passed across the city while you slept
The gatekeeper opens the East Gate
And the sun enters Babylon alone.
Put out the light.
These merchants will show you the way to your house.

Revolving Stage

Gold on the doorstep, whose steps
Nag the sand-drifts. Gold in the spittoon.
My father would sit on the steps emptying his shoe –
Pitchers of sand on each step.
If they went on they would lead nowhere,
But they lead back to my room.
Gold in a silver spoon,
My father's throat torn to sand.

I remember sneaking through the wings
To where the missing window hides me
From the audience and the looking glass.
If I looked back, trees were in bloom,
My father's album open on the floor,
Throbbing of bees in the lime.
His love of Spring was not in the photographs of the
    war,
But it burned his shoes and it buried him there.

Madonna of the Butterflies

On the stairs to the dormitories
I used to go past
A picture of the Virgin Mary
Made out of butterfly wings
Which cast a glow
Over the gloomy photographs
Of Field Marshal Earl Haig
And Admiral Jellicoe.
She has cast her friendly beams
Into the wilderness of my life.
I salute her in her solitude.

Hemlock

I have drawn up
All that is doubtful in the earth.
Mist gathers in my stem.

When I nod my head late at night
The air fills up with dust
And the books with ignorance.

Prayer while Sleeping

Brave blanket covering me
With a theme of arrows against the night,
Draw the coloured curtain tight,
Look after time for me.

Keep him satisfied while I sleep,
Slung like a bridge over this gorge,
This no-man's-land.
Keep him busy with his sand,
For I owe him emptiness.

LOVE-LIFE

(1979)

Once More with Feeling

My voice breaks
And I know it must be time
To pour out my heart to you again.

I would like to make you cry this once
but you smile encouragingly
Pleased to understand

Now and Again

We lift the bamboo curtain to the old hothouse
We see the upturned faces of our guests
They are smiling patiently
As if they have been expecting us
They sign to us to approach.

It is now that your cell blows across my face
As we move towards the table for the feast
We cut the cake like this,
Holding the knife and wishing for different things
They drink to our happiness.

Bar Italia

to T.S.

This is how we met,
Sheltering from work in this crowded coffee bar
This is where we sit
Propped at some narrow shelf

191

Once More with Feeling

My voice breaks
And I know it must be time
To pour out my heart to you again.

I would like to make you cry this once,
But you smile encouragingly,
Prepared to understand.

Now and Again

We lift the bamboo curtain to the old hothouse.
We see the upturned faces of our guests.
They are smiling patiently
As if they have been expecting us.
They sign to us to approach.

It is now that your veil blows across my face
As we move towards the table for the feast.
We cut the cake like this,
Holding the knife and wishing for different things.
They drink to our happiness.

Bar Italia
to L.S.

This is how we met,
Sheltering from work in this crowded coffee bar.
This is where we sit,
Propped at some narrow shelf,

Each day more crowded than the last
With undesirables.

I wish we could meet again
In two years' time,
Somewhere expensive where they remembered us
From the early days, before the crash.
Instead of here, instead of now,
Facing our reflections in the Bar Italia.

You would be frowning of course,
After all this time,
But then you would hold out your hand and say,
'Well, where are your three pages?'

I haven't written them. One day I will.
Anywhere but here it might seem possible.

Kites

Our lives fly well – white specks with faces
Running out against blue, while far below
We stand staring after them,
Trying to remember what they were like,
These prize possessions of ours,
Unravelling so cheerfully before our eyes.

By now we are winding in the runaway spools
For all we are worth. Whatever was there
Has begun to recede, like the dead stars,
Faster than the speed of their light
Reaches back to us here,
Where we hang on these empty strings.

Tides

The evening advances, then withdraws again
Leaving our cups and books like islands on the floor.
We are drifting you and I,
As far from one another as the young heroes
Of these two novels we have just laid down.
For that is happiness: to wander alone
Surrounded by the same moon, whose tides remind
    us of ourselves,
Our distances, and what we leave behind.
The lamp left on, the curtains letting in the light.
These things were promises. No doubt we will come
    back to them.

Impotence

You see me with my suits, my well-cut suits:
Past, present and future
Ranged close at hand upon their hooks.

How you hated them, hanging there so like me they hurt,
The herringbones, the faint chalk stripes,
Withdrawn from the wear and tear.

They were never in the wrong, the multi-pocketed,
The stay-at-homes. They were cosy-warm,
Huddling together there.

But where did you go that night
While I hung about upstairs, unwell, unable to decide,
Should I wear this one? Or that?
Take off the tie, or keep the waistcoat on?

You couldn't wait
When time ran out on me. I crossed the floor too late
To shut the cupboard which contained the sea.

Bachelors

What do they know of love
These men who have never been married?
What do they know
About living face to face with happiness
These amateurs of passion?
Do they imagine it's like home used to be,
Having a family of one's own,
Watching the little bones grow lethal,
The eyes turned on you –
And realizing suddenly that it's all
Your own fault the way things are,
Because it's you now
Not your parents who're in charge?
Can they understand what it means,
These suntanned single men? Or are they into cars?

And what do they know about the bedside lamp,
These denimed Romeos,
Its sphere of influence as night descends,
Familiar switch to hand:
On-off, off-on, the thousand little clicks
Half in, half out of the dark,
As the row gets going on time, or nothing does,
Or the bulb just sings to itself
On your side of the bed?
Pride in anger. That's your happiness.

A poisonous seed washed up with you
On a desert island of your own making,
Your impotence in flower like a hothouse rose.
And they talk about love
These men who have never been married.

Come, Tears

The days are full of darkness, the evenings glow
With longing for a year
That's going out. Come, night,
Fall fast on this house. Let me sleep
In love with her again. Come, tears, and fall
For other nights like this,
Whose spell I broke by so deceiving her.

Rain hissing at the window, the world is stuck
In the last groove of a year
That's nearly gone. Come, rain,
Splash your brushstrokes down
Grey stone. Come, tears, why don't you fall like that
On my hands, that I may find
This sadness no harder to bear?

A New Page

I write your name on a new sheet
To see if it will stand my weight.
It zig-zags like a crack
On the frozen surface of a lake

Which will only bear me up so long
As I keep moving.

A thousand unseen weaknesses
Turn foggy as they pluck like kisses
At thin ice. Uncertain territory
Stretches ahead, while behind me
A delta of tiny breakages begins
To scatter its reasons
Why I never can go back –
These words collapsing in my wake.

I should know where I am
By now in this pocket snowstorm
Shaken by a child, whose hands hold
A little snow-filled world
Up to the light
To see me struggling to stay upright
In her story. But I am lost
In a patch of weather from the past.

Familiar shadows queue
To usher in old promises, while through
The mist I see your ice-locked eyes
Looking back at me from these
Same sentences. I wonder will
They ever tire of their vigil.

Their longed-for colours of tenderness,
Changing to those of glass
Without warning, are still known only
To themselves, whose treachery
Was my own. Now that the page
Is covered with words in your image,

Will your heart melt? Will you break
The ice between us, for my sake?

Your Way Home

I turn my back on you and have to watch the cars
Competing on the rain-washed motorway. Only the
     rain
And a line of poplar trees which seems to end
At this rustic slum of ours can point
To why we huddle here, in the middle-distance,
     shivering.

When I shout at you to leave me on my own
You know very well what I mean, but you don't come
     near.
For once you just do as I say – your suitcases
Clenched tight round property and the past. I could
     weep
For showing so little strength with you.

In the lull, I can hear the poplar trees
Pouring on wind such ecstasy as we have known
In this old barn with beds for furniture,
Hearing the rain on the sloping roof all night,
Not hoping it would stop or let us go.

Tonight the same night is drawing in its colours, now
As then, though we of that night are not the same.
And nature can do nothing more for us this time
Than count the hours till you must find your way
Back from this place and start to live again.

Your absence falls in front of you. Your gestures have
    withdrawn
Almost to the horizon, where rain, filed thin,
Floats in across the miles of flood-fed earth
That will come between us. I can see your car
Move up the slip-road into the London lane.

Broken Dreams

The women sleep.
We look for them in their dreams.

When we bump into a piece of the scenery,
It falls, waking them.

They open eyes full of broken love.
Love that we have broken.

The White Hair

Last thing, I take my walk
Through streets I know too well for walking in.
The lamplight over-reaches my steps, as days
Lap one another's memories.
How precious to me now
The word 'I' would be on your lips.

The hungry hours of the earth grope through me
In their search for images.
I wish I could pluck you out of me
As easily as the white hair I saw in the mirror,

Though even then I noticed my searching right hand
Start moving in the wrong direction.

Along These Lines

And so you cry for her, and the poem falls to the page
As if it knew all along that what we make of ourselves
    we take
From one another's hearts – tearing and shouting until
    we learn
How awkwardly, upstairs and behind shut doors we
    are born,
Already owing interest on what we have borrowed
    from the world.

The Ribbon

I thought she'd taken all her things
But I was wrong. Wherever I go
I catch glimpses of my damnation.

Is that too strong a word? You wouldn't think so
If you could see this lovely ribbon
Wound around my hand.

Don't tell me, I know,
I'm mumbling to myself again. I'm like King Kong
Picking among the ruins of New York
For a clue to his misfortune.

[83]

I keep wondering what they were like,
These odds and ends,
Collecting dust, though freed at last from blame.
Did they look the same
When she held them in her hand?

It seems ridiculous
How everything here acknowledges her touch,
Including me, including this tangled ribbon.

Perhaps you were right after all
And I make too much of it. I'll just sit here now
And try to undo these knots –
I'll be with you in a minute, if you can wait.

Stagefright

thinking of my father

Dazed with the sadness of lost things
In ordered silence
I sat down in the dining room for tea:
Biscuits and a glass of Moselle, no radio.
(How kind we are to ourselves!)
And I tried to imagine
What he would have done at a time like this.
For I will say this,
He knew what to do in an emergency
And he knew what to drink.
So I put some more wine in the fridge
And I hurried round to her house.
I shouted her name and knocked
But she spoke to me through the frosted glass

And I'm glad I couldn't see her face
When she told me it was all over between us.

Then I shivered like a man with stagefright
And I watched the world
Come slowly to a standstill before my eyes:
The sinking of the heart.
It seemed unacceptable suddenly
To be walking the streets on such a night
With love like so much small change
Left over from a pound.
I could hear him telling me:
'Women are strong, but they fall
Like sleep from your eyes. Let your step
Spring on the sidewalk and you'll see
Your only fault's unhappiness.'
Then I came back here and got into my good suit,
Having chucked the biscuits
And opened the bottle of wine.

Present Continuous

Well, I am still
The unofficial guardian of your house,
Which is not your house any more,
And not the same place we trusted to be there
Whenever we came home.
Our possessions lie
Abandoned, back along the way:
These books, those dresses under cellophane.
I haven't moved
Your plastic carrier bags from the hall

And fifty pairs of shoes
Still hang around the window on the stairs,
The changing fashions of your years with me.

After the Show

It's been too long since I waited up for you
With something to eat after the show
And everything done.
Too long since I sat here with a grin
While the bloody show moved on.

As if to remind me,
The news comes round again
About a famous ballet star's defection.
By midnight, she is blond and beautiful
And there is a man in her life.

Are you blond and beautiful at last?
Or don't you care?
When people ask after you I have no news for them
Except that you are far away from here
And everything is forgiven.
I wonder how they went, those simple nights,
Before the years set in.

Love at Night

She is with me now, my lifelong visitor,
She who has faithfully instructed me
In the art of being alone. She will not rest

Till she has taught me all there is to love
And left me here to learn the facts by heart.

Even now, she is undressing in her mirror
While I lie here, awaiting tonight's lesson
On how to exist without her another hour.
I know what she will say: 'Don't look at me.
I feel guilty coming here like this
After so long. I don't know what to do.'

See how gently she has persuaded me
That every night I spend with her is my last.
Merciless angel, it has been your task
To teach me how to live without you finally.

Good

When the record slides to a close
I imagine your key in the lock,
Your handlebars bumping against the wall
You are so angry to be back.

Look – you have still got me
Gliding about your business as before.
Wherever you are out there, in the cold night air,
You would be proud of me.
I've never been so good.

Confessions of a Drifter

I used to sell perfume in the New Towns.
I was popular in the saloons.
Professional women slept in my trailer.
Young salesgirls broke my heart. For ten years
I never went near our Main Office.

From shop to shop
And then from door to door I went
In a slowly diminishing circle of enchantment
With 'Soir de Paris' and 'Flower of the Orient'.

I used up all my good luck
Wetting the wrists of teenagers in bars
With 'English Rose' and 'Afro-Dizziac'
From giveaway dispensers.

From girl to girl
And then from bar to bar I went
In a slowly expanding circle
Of liquid replenishment.

I would park my trailer outside a door
So I could find it when I walked out of there,
Throwing back my shoulders at the night – a hero
To myself.

They knock on my window this morning. Too late
I wake out of my salesman's paradise,
The sperm drying on my thigh
And nothing but the name of a drifter in the New
    Towns.

Love-Life

Her veil blows across my face
As we cling together in the porch.
Propped on the mantelpiece,
The photograph distils our ecstasy.
Each night we touch
The heart-shaped frame of our reliquary
And sigh for love.

Each morning we are young again –
Our cheeks brushed pink,
The highlights in our hair.
Our guests will be arriving soon.
We wait contentedly beyond the glass
For them to find us here,
Our smiles wrapped in lace.

WRITING HOME

(1985)

At Least a Hundred Words

What shall we say in our letters home?
That we're perfectly all right?
That we stand on the playground with red faces
and our hair sticking up?
That we give people Chinese burns?
Mr Ray, standing in the entrance to the lavatories
with his clipboard and pen,
turned us round by our heads
and gave us a boot up the arse.
We can't put that in our letters home
because Mr Ray is taking letter-writing.
He sits in his master's chair
winding the propeller of his balsa wood aeroplane
with a glue-caked index finger
and looking straight ahead.
RESULTS OF THE MATCH, DESCRIPTION OF THE FLOODS,
THE LECTURE ON KENYA, UGANDA AND TANGANYIKA
WITH COLOUR SLIDES AND HEADDRESSES.
We have to write at least a hundred words
to the satisfaction of Mr Ray
before we can go in to tea,
so I put up my hand to ask if we can count the 'ands'.
Mr Ray lets go the propeller of his Prestwick 'Pioneer'
and it unwinds with a long drawn-out sigh.
He'd rather be out overflying
enemy territory on remote
than 'ministering to the natives' in backward C4.
He was shot down in World War One or World War
Two, he forgets,
but it didn't do him a damn bit of harm.
It made a man of him.

He goes and stands in the corner near the door
and offers up his usual prayer:
'One two three four five six seven
God give me strength to carry on.'
While his back is turned
I roll a marble along the groove in the top of my desk
till it drops through the inkwell
on to the track I've made for it inside. I can hear it
travelling round the system of books
and rulers: a tip-balance, then a spiral,
then a thirty-year gap as it falls through
the dust-hole into my waiting hand.

Just Another Day

When you were young
you came downstairs in the middle of the night
and saw the living room.
The furniture lay about your feet.
The carpet had been folded back
where it met the skirting board.

You opened the front door
and stood for a moment on the step.
Little pieces of metal
shone in the asphalt on the road.
The chimneys were pot-bellied apostles
preaching to the stars.

You cleared your throat, or coughed,
and the dawn chorus started up –
excited by an item of news

which might have been you,
or might have been just another day.
You stood there for a moment, listening.

Before the War

'You should have been there then,' they tell you,
the girls who were there themselves.
'Before the war,
your father was the kind of man
to take you, on the spur of a telegram,
to one of those Continental casinos
where they keep the curtains drawn
all summer: white ties and Sidney Bechet,
gardenias on a breakfast tray.
You'd follow the road-map south
in someone's aeroplane,
putting down in a field while it was light.
Oh, those were the days all right,
and the nights too for someone like your father.'

Then you mourn the fact once more
that you missed knowing him then,
that you hardly recognize this man
who somehow jumped the gun
and started ahead of you. It isn't fair,
but there's nothing to be done. The casinos are dead
and the nights are drawing in.
Though you follow the road-map south
on the spur of a lifetime
you'll never catch up with the fun
and he won't be back for you.

You're strung out like runners
across the world, losing ground,
in a race that began when you were born.

A Walking Gentleman

I started very slowly,
being rude to everybody
and going home early
without really knowing why.
I carried on that way
till my father died
and allowed me to grow my hair.
I didn't want to any more.
I came through a side door,
my hands slightly raised,
as if whatever was going on
needed lifting by me.
I bought a clove carnation
in Moyses Stevens
and cut the sepals off
and forced the whole thing
through my buttonhole
till it lay flat against the lapel
like a brooch, not a bouquet.
I walked all the way up Piccadilly
to the top of the Haymarket,
stopping every so often.
Surely Scott's is somewhere near here?
I can't see it any more.
My feet are hurting me.

Waiting to Go On

I turned the pages slowly, listening for the car,
till my father was young again, a soldier,
or throwing back his head
on slicked-back Derby Days before the war.
I stared at all that fame and handsomeness
and thought they were the same.
Good looks were everything where I came from.
They made you laugh. They made you have a tan.
They made you speak with conviction.
'Such a nice young man!' my mother used to say.
'So good looking!' Left alone in the house,
I searched my face for signs of excellence,
turning up my collar in the long mirror on the stairs
and flourishing a dress sword at myself:
'Hugh Williams, even more handsome in Regency!'
The sound of wheels on the drive
meant I had about one minute
to put everything back where I'd found it
and come downstairs as myself.

Tipping My Chair

I shivered in 1958. I caught a glimpse
of money working and I shut my eyes.
I was a love-sick crammer-candidate, reading
poetry under the desk in History,
wondering how to go about my life.
'Write a novel!' said my father.
'Put everything in! Sell the film rights for a fortune!

Sit up straight!' I sat there, filleting
a chestnut leaf in my lap, not listening.
I wanted to do nothing, urgently.

At his desk, in his dressing-gown,
among compliant womenfolk, he seemed
too masterful, too horrified by me.
He banged the table if I tipped my chair.
He couldn't stand my hair. One day,
struggling with a chestnut leaf, I fell over backwards
or the chair-leg broke. I didn't care any more
if poetry was easier than prose. I lay there
in the ruins of a perfectly good chair
and opened my eyes. I knew what I didn't want to do.

At his desk, in his dressing-room, among
these photographs of my father in costume,
I wonder how to go about his life.
Put everything in? The bankruptcy? The hell?
The little cork-and-leather theatrical
'lifts' he used to wear? The blacking for his hair?
Or again: leave everything out? Do nothing,
tip my chair back and stare at him for once,
my lip trembling at forty?
My father bangs the table: 'Sit up straight!'

A Little While Longer

My father stands at an angle
to the Church of St Ethelburga in the City,
the divorcees' church.
My mother hangs back,
shielding her eyes from the flashes.
She twists her new ring,
while my father explains to reporters
how something unwinds in mid-air –
a marriage perhaps,
or could it be a googly?
His knuckles show white
on the officer's swagger stick
which he's holding like a kite reel.
Why clench thy fists, O little one?
Thy mother's near and sure there's none
would wish to fight thee.
The reporters laugh uneasily,
remembering to mention
the children of a previous marriage,
their ages and places of birth.
They've asked him to smile
and he's twisted his moustache for them.
His seedy, civilian best man
tries to pull him away to the reception.

An Actor's War

Tunisia, 1943

'It is difficult to assess the value of the part played by the
organisation known as Phantom during this stage of our
operations in North Africa.'
Official History of the Second World War

> Before the British public
> I was once a leading man.
> Now behind a British private
> I just follow, if I can.
> Hugh Williams

March

Well, here we are in our Tropical Kit –
shirts and shorts and little black toques,
looking like a lot of hikers or cyclists
with dead bluebells on the handlebars.
It seems we have at last discovered a place
where it is impossible to spend money. What a pity
that it should be a rather muddy wadi
in Tunisia, where whisky is prohibited by God.
How sorry I am that I ever said an unkind word
about the Palmer's Arms. In my nostalgia
it seems the very Elysium of Alcohol.
I can imagine you in about an hour
pattering round to meet your beaux.
The last couple of days I've realized with a bang
what an appalling time this bloody war has been on.
Three and a half years last night
since we walked out of the stage door of the Queen's Theatre
into the Queen's Westminsters.
What good times we had. But it all seems
a long time ago, looking back, doesn't it?

April

Early morning – or what in happier times
was late at night. Strong and sweet black coffee,
laced with the last little drop out of my flask,
has reminded me of that stuff they used to serve
on fire inside a coconut at The Beachcomber
to put the finishing touches to a Zombie.
I'm still floundering in the work here.
I lie awake sometimes wondering if my map
is marked correctly. I lose notebooks
and have to rely on little bits of paper.
Benzedrine tablets, please. Chemist next to the Pavilion.
A kiss and a lump of chocolate for Hugo
for being able to walk.
Please God he never has to march.

May

It's all very green down here at the moment –
lots of wild flowers and lots of your gum trees
with their barks hanging down like tattered lingerie.
I saw a stork flying and heard a lark singing
as though he were over Goodwood racecourse
on that wonderful day when Epigram won the Cup
and you won me. The villages look like those
in Provence and the milestones with little red tops
make me long for the days to come
when you and I are scuttling down the Route Bleue
in search of sunshine and eights and nines.*
Having taken trouble all one's life to seek pleasure,
to find now that delights are down to a canvas bath

* The good cards in Chemmy.

taken with one's legs hanging over the side in a bucket,
is strange, though no doubt good for one.
I dare say I shall be pretty bloody exquisite
for quite some time after the war – silks and lotions
and long sessions at the barber
and never again will a red carnation be made to last
from lunchtime until the following dawn.
When the war is over I intend no longer
to practise this foolish and half-hearted method
of letting money slip through my fingers.
I intend in future to allow it to pour
in great torrents from my pockets.
Don't be alarmed. This is only the talk of a man
with mosquito lotion on his face and hands
and anti-louse powder in the seams of his clothes,
who drinks his highly medicated morning tea
from a tin mug with shaving soap round the rim
and uses gum boots for bedroom slippers.

June

Writing by our Mediterranean now, but the wrong bank.
The same sunshine and azure sea, a few of the same
flowers and trees and the purple bougainvillea,
but there it ends. Enough to make one want more –
a bottle cooling in a pool,
a yellow bathing dress drying on a rock.
Perhaps if we fight on we shall arrive in a country
where there is something fit to drink.
How pleasant to be advancing through the Côte d'Or
with one's water bottle filled with Pouilly.
Instead of which we're stuck in this blasted cork forest
learning to kill flies.

Sometimes it seems we love England
more than each other, the things we do for her.
I wonder if, when it's over, we'll be glad.
Or shall we think I was a fool to sacrifice so much?
Oh God, we'll be glad, won't we? I don't know.
Not on this damned dust hurricane I don't.
But if you love me I shan't care.
You and Hugo have a coating of desert on your faces.
I must wipe you.

July

The battle – if one can dignify such a shambles –
is closed in this sector and there is an atmosphere
of emptying the ashtrays and counting the broken
    glasses.
Churchill arrived to address the First Army
in the Roman Amphitheatre at Carthage.
He looked like a Disney or Beatrix Potter creature
and spoke without his teeth. Cigar, V-sign, all the tricks,
and I thought of that day outside the Palace
with Chamberlain smiling peace with honour
and we kidded ourselves there was a chance –
two little suckers so in love
and so longing for a tranquil sunny life.

August

How's my boy? Shirts and trousers!
Poor little Hawes and Curtis. Another year or so
and our accounts will be getting muddled
and I shall find myself getting involved
in white waistcoats I've never seen.
Tell him to pay cash. Go and tell him now.

The thought terrifies me.
Have been harassed lately by the old divided duties –
the only part of the war I can honestly say
has been bloody. Maybe the cinema racket
gives one the wrong impression of one's worth,
but I sometimes feel I'd be better employed at Denham
as Captain Daring R.N. than housekeeping for Phantom.
Stupid, for one must do one or the other
and not attempt both as I have done.
Had a letter from the Income Tax
asking for some quite ridiculous sum.
Next time you see Lil tell her to write and say
I'm unlikely to be traceable
until quite some time after the war, if then.
I think when I die I should like my ashes
blown through the keyhole of the Treasury
in lieu of further payments.
My wages here are roughly what it used to cost me
to look after my top hat before the war.
Flog it, by all means. I can't see that kind of thing
being any use after the war, unless it's for comedy.
Did some Shakespeare at the Hospital Concert
the other night and was nervous as a cat.
God knows what a London first night will be like
with all the knockers out front, waiting and hoping.
I doubt if I'll make it. Sometimes I really doubt it.
I'll probably run screaming from the theatre
just as they call the first quarter.
Tell the girls to keep on with Puck and the First Fairy
as I shall want to see it when I come home.

September

Had a deadly exercise down on the plain last week
and the blasted Arabs stole my lavatory seat.
Medals should be given for exercises, not campaigns.
One would have the Spartan Star for Needless Discomfort
in the face of Overwhelming Boredom.
I had to give a cheque for £48 to Peter Baker
and I doubt there's that much in my account.
Now he's going home by air because of an appendix
and taking the cheque with him.
I couldn't be sorrier to do this to you once again,
but his appendix took me by surprise, as it did him.
Tell Connie I must have a picture before Christmas.

October

Every known kind of delay and disappointment
has attended us and I am filled with a sulky despair
and a general loathing for mankind.
People are so bored they have started growing
and shaving off moustaches, a sure sign
of utter moral decay. I have luckily made friends
with a little fellow who keeps me supplied
with a sufficiency of Algerian brandy,
so I expect the major part of my waking life
to be spent in pain and hangover.
Added to all other horrors,
Christmas Theatricals have cropped up,
which really has crowned my ultimate unhappiness.
Perhaps if I tell you that after
an hour and a half of forceful argument
I have just succeeded in squashing an idea

to produce an abbreviated version of Midsummer Night's
   Dream
by the end of the week – without wigs, costumes,
stage or lighting and only one copy of the play,
you will appreciate the nervous exhaustion I suffer.
The idea of acting is rich. Not for a line of this letter
have I avoided making those aimless
slightly crazy-looking gestures to remove the flies.
I have a mug of tea and there must be thirty round the brim.
I can kill them now by flicking them,
as opposed to banging oneself all over.
I think they must be slower down here,
for I can't believe that I am quicker.

As I Went to Sleep

At last he was coming home, whoever he was.
In a couple of weeks we'd be hearing the telephone
and Sally's boyfriend would be going home to America.

I put my ear to the humming telephone poles
and intercepted my father's messages.
I sent him messages in my prayers,

then Sally's boyfriend moved my cot out into the hall
and slipped some chewing gum under my pillow
to keep my mouth shut. The smell of spearmint

made my mouth water. As I went to sleep
I could hear them calling one another's name
as if they were already miles apart.

Tangerines

'Before the war' was once-upon-a-time
by 1947. I had to peer through cigarette smoke
to see my parents in black and white
lounging on zebra skins, while doormen stood by doors
in pale grey uniforms.

I wished I was alive before the war
when Tony and Mike rode their bicycles into the lake,
but after the war was where I had to stay,
upstairs in the nursery, with Nanny
and the rocking-horse. It sounded more fun
to dance all night and fly to France for breakfast.
But after the war I had to go to bed.

In my prisoner's pyjamas. I looked through
banisters into that polished, pre-war place
where my parents lived. If I leaned out
I could see the elephant's foot
tortured with shooting sticks
and a round mirror which filled from time to time
with hats and coats and shouts,
then emptied like a bath.

Every summer my parents got in the car
and drove back through the war to the South of France.
I longed to go with them, but I was stuck
in 1948 with Nanny Monkenbeck.

They sent me sword-shaped eucalyptus leaves
and purple, pre-war flowers, pressed
between the pages of my first letters. One year
a box of tangerines arrived for me from France.

I hid behind the sofa in my parents' bedroom,
eating my way south to join them.

Slow Train

My father let the leather window-strap
slip through his fingers and I smelt the sea.
He was showing me gun emplacements
to stop me feeling train-sick
on our first holiday after the war.
I clutched my new bucket in two lifeless hands,
excited by the blockhouse
which had exploded, killing everyone.
We went over a bridge he had guarded
and he lit two cigarettes and threw them down
to some soldiers cutting barbed wire.
He said there was something fast for me
in the guard's van, if I could hang on.
I sat there, staring at one of the holes
in the window-strap, imagining death
as a sort of surprise for men in uniform.
'I-think-I-can-I-think-I-can'
the train was supposed to be saying
as we came to Dungeness Lighthouse in the dark,
but I didn't think I could.
When we started going backwards, I was glad.

New Coat, Last Chance

I wore a coat like this
when they rescued me from the plot
of my first adventure.

I was climbing the weir with my dog.
'Don't move!' shouted my governess
from the prow of a motorboat.

I washed my hands in the vestry,
but the smell of oilskin
stayed on my fingers in church.

My disgrace comes back to me
as I turn up the collar
in the long mirror of this shop.

'Don't move!' whispers my governess.
Her goggles freeze me in my tracks.
My feet slither.

Smells remember us as we were then –
half fact, half fiction –
trying on different lives.

They race ahead of us like spaniels,
turning and waiting by a river
for their masters to come true.

Walking Out of the Room Backwards

Out of work at fifty, smoking fifty a day,
my father wore his sheepskin coat

and went to auditions
for the first time in his life.
I watched in horror from my bedroom window
as he missed the bus to London
in full view of the house opposite.
'If it weren't for you and the children',
he told my mother from his bed,
'I'd never get up in the morning.'

He wasn't amused
when I burst in on his sleep
with a head hollowed out of a turnip
swinging from a broom. There were cigarette burns
like bullet-holes in his pyjamas.
I saw his bad foot
sticking out from under the bedclothes
because he was 'broke'
and I thought my father was dying.
I wanted to make him laugh, but I got it wrong
and only frightened myself.

The future stands behind us, holding ready
a chloroform-soaked handkerchief.
The past stretches ahead, into which we stare,
as into the eyes of our parents
on their wedding day –
shouting something from the crowd
or waving things on sticks
to make them look at us. To punish me,
or amuse his theatrical friends,
my father made me walk out of the room backwards,
bowing and saying, 'Goodnight, my liege.'

Leaving School

I was eight when I set out into the world
wearing a grey flannel suit.
I had my own suitcase.
I thought it was going to be fun.
I wasn't listening
when everything was explained to us in the Library,
so the first night I didn't have any sheets.
The headmaster's wife told me
to think of the timetable as a game of 'Battleships'.
She found me walking around upstairs
wearing the wrong shoes.

I liked all the waiting we had to do at school,
but I didn't like the work.
I could only read certain things
which I'd read before, like the Billy Goat Gruff books,
but they didn't have them there.
They had the Beacon Series.
I said 'I don't know,'
then I started saying nothing.
Every day my name was read out
because I'd forgotten to hang something up.

I was so far away from home I used to forget things.
I forgot how to get undressed.
You're supposed to take off your shirt and vest
after you've put on your pyjamas bottoms.
When the headmaster's wife came round for Inspection
I was fully dressed again, ready for bed.
She had my toothbrush in her hand
and she wanted to know why it was dry.
I was miles away, with my suitcase, leaving school.

Scratches

My mother scratched the soles of my shoes
to stop me slipping
when I went away to school.

I didn't think a few scratches
with a pair of scissors
was going to be enough.

I was walking on ice,
my arms stretched out.
I didn't know where I was going.

Her scratches soon disappeared
when I started sliding
down those polished corridors.

I slid into class.
I slid across the hall into the changing-room.
I never slipped up.

I learnt how to skate along with an aeroplane
or a car, looking ordinary,
pretending to have fun.

I learnt how long a run I needed
to carry me as far as the gym
in time for Assembly.

I turned as I went,
my arms stretched out to catch the door jamb
as I went flying past.

When Will His Stupid Head Remember?

Mr Ray stood behind me in History,
waiting for me to make a slip.
I had to write out the Kings and Queens
of England, in reverse order, with dates. I put,
'William I, 1087–1066'. I could smell the aeroplane glue
on his fingers as he took hold of my ear.
I stood in the corner near the insect case,
remembering my bike. I had the John Bull
Puncture Repair Kit in my pocket: glass paper,
rubber solution, patches, chalk and grater,
spare valves. I was 'riding dead' –
freewheeling downhill with my arms folded
and my eyes shut, looking Mr Ray in the eye.
Every time I looked round he added a minute to my
    sentence.

Mr Ray held his red Biro Minor like a modelling knife
to write reports. He drew a wooden spoon.*
'I found it hard to keep my temper
with this feeble and incompetent creature.
He was always last to find his place
and most of his questions had been answered
five minutes before . . .' I called my father 'sir'
when he opened the envelope and shouted.
I was practising stage-falls from my bike
in the fading spotlight of summer lawns,
remembering the smell of aeroplane glue and inkwells
with a shiver down my spine. The beginning of term
was creeping up on me. Every time I looked round
Mr Ray was standing there, stockstill.

* 'bottom of the class'

A Letter to My Parents

There is quite a lot of news from this front.
I got hit in the face, but I am all right now.
How are you? How is the play?
A little dog called Bobby ran out into the road
and was run over by a car.
I am sorry this is in pencil, but I am upstairs
lying down. I am in the same room as last term
but my bed is next to my old one
and bang next to the door.
Roberts is sleeping in my old bed.
We are going to have a gang, so we sign our name in
    blood.
We have to have sunray treatment
which seems a complete waste of time.
We had a lecture on the Headhunters of Borneo.
The Headhunters are in the literal sense.
They cut off your head
and cut off all your hair
and play football with your skull.
Or else they bash up all your brains and pour hot sand
in through your neck, until it shrinks
and they paint it blue.
Then afterwards we played charades with the man.
There were two old people in India
and the door had blown open.
'First to speak closes the door,' said the man.
Then in the morning the woman had to speak.
'Woman, you have spoken. Close the door.'
Didn't one of our relations
used to be the ruler of Borneo?
I said he did, but the man wasn't sure.

I will tell you about charades in more detail
when you come down.
Could you bring some decorations with you?
And one or two of your plays that you don't really
    want?
I am sending the going out days for you to fill in.
Apparently there is a map, or you could ask.

Heroes of the Sub-Plot

Look at us, cursed heroes of the sub-plot,
twisting our faces into plaintive masks
over the footlights – terror, desire and glee.
For we are lost, as usual at this hour,
in a wood near the front of the stage –
cuckolds and clowns and palace functionaries,
rolling our eyes to pass the time for you
with one or two approved cross purposes.
See – we have put on character make-up
to distract you from the sound of scenery
being shifted behind our backs. The principals
are waiting in the wings. Too soon
our leading man will make the winding sign
to end our moment balanced in the light.
We smudge our eye-shadow with our tears.

Shelf-Life

Above our beds
the little wooden shelf
with one support
was like a crucifix
offering up
its hairbrush, Bible,
family photograph
for trial by mockery.

We lay in its shadow
on summer nights,
denying everything,
hearing only
the impossible high catches
for the older boys,
their famous surnames
calling them to glory.

2

Why did we take
the bed-making competition
so seriously?
We were only nine.
We measured our turndowns
with a ruler.
We used a protractor
to fix the angle of our
hospital corners
at forty-five degrees.

Our shelves were identical.
Our Bibles lay
on their sides, facing in.
Our hairbrushes lay on their backs
with a comb stuck in them.
If anyone's hairbrush had a handle
they had to hide it
in their dressing-gown
and borrow a proper one
for the competition.

In the centre of our shelves
stood our photo-frame,
a difficult area
that couldn't be tidied away
or forgiven. By the time we had
solved the problem
of our counterpane
our parents were looking
straight past one another
into opposite corners of the room.

3

Their smiles were
lost on us
and ours on them,
as if they were still
waving goodbye to the wrong
upstairs window
from the car.
In their long absence,
our double photo-frame

was a bedtime
story-book,
propped open like a trap
at the pictures.

We said to ourselves,
'Brothers and sisters
have I none,
but this man's father
is my father's son.
Who am I?' –
holding our fingers
on our father's
encouraging smile
and repeating it
over to ourselves
till we started
to lose our place.

4

I knew it wasn't my father
who was bankrupt and poor.
He had a war.
He had a scar.
He was on Famous Film Star
Cigarette Cards
with Janet Gaynor.
It couldn't be my father
who hit the registrar
and had to be bound over for a year
to keep the peace,
so who were they talking about
in the newspaper?

[118]

If he was famous,
why hadn't I heard of him?

He looked uncertain
in the signed
photograph on my shelf
that was attracting
too much attention
for my own good.
His hair was perfection.
His eyes were fixed on the horizon
where something vaguely
troublesome was going on
behind my back.
The smoke from his cigarette
had been touched in
against a background
of pleated satin.

5

I found his name
in the Library *Who's Who*
and tore the page out
hoping it would say.
I memorized dozens
of forgotten films and plays
to prove my father
innocent of bankruptcy.
His brief biography
was followed by a personal note:
'Clubs: none, Sports: none,
Hobbies: none.
Address: c/o *Spotlight*.'

[119]

I tried to explain
that the German
bubble-car
in the photograph
of our house
was part of
a Spitfire
my father had flown
in the war.
The swastikas
on my blanket
were ancient
symbols of fortune
the other way round.

I sat in bed
tracing the faces
of my parents
on lavatory paper.
Riddles and smut
poured from their lips
in my defence,
but the evidence
was attached to
a blind-cord.
Up it flew,
hoisting my shit-
stained underpants
into full view.

A Life of Crime

If I got into trouble I was to go to him
and tell him everything.
It didn't matter if I was unhappy, or in love,
or wanted by the police. I could say,
'Daddy, I've killed a Chinaman'
and he'd see what he could do.

He gave me a knife for my birthday
and I cut my hand on it
and flung it away into the long grass,
running after it in vain
as it started to disappear
over the horizon of the lawn.

It was easy to imagine myself
finding the knife and wearing it on a chain
the way he had shown me,
but not so easy when the grass had grown
and been cut many times,
the garden gone next door.

I must have been looking too far away
or I must have been looking too near.
A wealth of personal detail
accumulates in folders, like a life of crime,
but nothing conclusive,
nothing to get arrested for.

Snorkel

to my brother

You carried the rattans and the towels.
I carried the windshield
and one of the old snorkels
with ping-pong balls for valves.

What happened to the other one
with yellow glass, the one that was dangerous?
We both wanted that one.
It didn't mist up. We slung ourselves

half way between heaven and earth
that summer – holding our breath
and diving for sand-dollars.
If we breathed out all the air in our lungs

we could grab another ten seconds
on the sea-bed. We spent half our lives
waiting for each other to come out of the water
so we could have our turn.

New Ground

We played Scrabble wrong for years.
We counted the Double and Triple Word Scores
as often as we liked.
We had to move aside the letters
to see what colours they were on.

My father was out of work
and we were moving again. He stared at the board,

twisting his signet ring.
He liked adding 's' to a word
and scoring more points
than the person who thought of it.
If you needed a word badly enough
you had a right to it.

My father wanted 'chinas'.
He said they were ornamental
bricks from Derbyshire, hand-painted.
He cheated from principle, to open up
new ground for his family.
Not 'God feeds the ravens' so much
as 'The world is my country'. We were stuck

at the end of a lane in Sussex
for two winters. My father threw down
his high-scoring spelling mistakes and bluffs
and started counting:
'aw' as in 'Aw, hell!', 'ex' with the 'x' falling
on the last Triple Letter Score.

Dégagé

Clothes were a kind of wit. You either
carried them off, or you looked ridiculous.
'Make a girl laugh,' said my father,
which I did. Whatever I put on
made me look even younger than my brother,
who was ten.

I tried every combination
of cravat and cardigan in my efforts to look

natural, *dégagé*. I dug my hand
into the pocket of my flannels
and felt the little rolls of pocket dust
under my fingernails – and remained a virgin.

My father's forty-seven suits
awaiting his pleasure in a separate dressing-room
were proof of his superior wit. Who else
had a white barathea dinner jacket
he never even wore, or turned-back cuffs
and no turn-ups on his trousers?

At fourteen I was nagging my grandmother
to make me shirts with fuller sleeves.
My jeans I wanted taken in *and* flared.
I was very keen on suede. 'You should be with someone
a full minute,' said my father,
'before you realize they're well dressed.'

I imagined it dawning on people
in sixty seconds flat
that I was his equal at last.
'Suppose you realize before that?' I asked,
wriggling my toes in my chisel-toed chukka boots.
'Probably queer,' said my father.

Making Friends with Ties

His khaki tie was perfectly knotted in wartime.
The tail was smartly plumped.
The dent became a groove
where it entered a sturdy, rectangular knot,
never a Windsor.

This groove came out
in exactly the same place all his life,
never in the middle,
but slightly to the left.
'You have to get it right first time,'
he told me, my first term at school.
'Otherwise you go raving mad.'

I was so impressed by this
I didn't listen in class.
I made friends with people's ties, not them.
One day when I was drunk I told him,
'I don't like the groove!'
His face softened towards me for a moment.
'Don't you, dear boy? Well, I'm *delighted*.'

Three Quarters

I wasn't happy with aspects of my case.
I shut myself in the bathroom,
a three-sided looking glass open like a book.
I couldn't understand my face. My nose stuck out.
I combed my hair down over my eyes
in search of a parting that would change my life.

I opened the mirror slowly, turning my head
from full to three-quarter face.
I wanted to stand three-quarters on to the world,
near the vanishing point.
I sat in front of the sunray lamp
with pennies in my eyes. I dyed my skin

a streaky, yellowish brown with permanganate of
  potash.
I must have grown up slowly
in that looking glass bathroom,
combing my hair straight down and pretending to
  wash.
I made myself dizzy raising my arms above my head
in a kind of surrender. No one else could get in.

Early Work

When I came downstairs my hair looked
  extraordinary –
a turmoil of popular styles and prejudices,
stiff with unreality and fear.
My scalp stung from onsets of a steel flick-comb.
My parting was raw from realignment.
I'd reintroduced the casual look so many times
I'd lost track of it completely. The whole thing
looked like an instrument of self-torture
with a handle and a zip.

I made my entrance and everyone wanted to know
where I was off to looking like that.
My brother did a comb mime with his knife,
tongue hanging out, jacket pushed back like a Ted.
My father made me go upstairs and start again.
I'd been working on my hair for so long
I thought it was natural to have a whirlpool
on your head, or a ship. I couldn't grasp the fact
that my hair was my hair, nothing more.

Raids on Lunch

Every lunchtime I came under threat
from my father's parting,
a venomous vapour trail
set at right angles to his profile.
I was the enemy,
po-faced and pale,
and armed with a sort of quiff.
'Ett, ett,' he snapped,
shooting down a joke,
when I made the mistake
of pronouncing 'ate'
as if it rhymed with 'late'.
I hated the way his jaw went slack
as he calmly demolished me.
I couldn't resist
saying something tasteless
about the Royal Air Force,
having seen him disguised as a nun
in *One of Our Aircraft is Missing*.
I should have run for cover.
Hooking a forefinger
over his much-admired nose
was the remains of my father's
camera-consciousness.
It meant he was critical:
the moment of sloth
before the nun takes off her headdress
and opens fire on the Nazis.

A Parting Shot

When I started going out
my father thought my hair should go straight back.
It grew straight forward.

He offered to wet it for me,
to train it back, like his. 'I used to have full lips
like yours when I was your age.'

We looked at each other
in the three-sided looking glass, ranks
of opposing profiles fanning out round the room.
His parting stood like a feather in his cap.

He laid his cigarette on the shelf
and started wetting my hair.
'For God's sake, GROW UP!' he shouted,
emptying the jug over my head.

The Spring of Sheep

Pro-Plus Rapid Energy Tablets
gave me Extra Vitality
when I visited my girlfriend on her father's stud.
The double-backing local bus
took two hours to travel twenty miles.
When it passed our house
I nearly got off by mistake.
I noticed a roof I hadn't been on
and wished I was up there with my gun.
My hands were shaking
as I thought of things to say:

how the enlargements had gone astray
and been pinned to the noticeboard,
how my tutor asked if it was Brigitte Bardot.
I practised laughing in the window of the bus,
but I laughed on the other side of my face
when I saw her riding her pony
in her Sloppy Joe.
We were sitting alone in the nursery,
waiting for her father's horse to appear on television.
My left hand felt numb,
but my right took leave of its senses
and set out for the unknown regions of her shoulders.
I watched through binoculars
as it lay there with altitude sickness.
If it was mine, how could I get it back in time
for dinner with her parents, bloodstock
and doping scandals? A gong
sounded somewhere in the house
and I leapt to my feet. Everyone was proud
of the gallant Cigarette Case
and my girlfriend ran over to the stables
to say goodnight. Head-over-heels with Pro-Plus,
I lay awake for hours, experiencing fierce
but tender feelings for the mattress
in a spare room hung with antique jigsaws:
'Les Generaux en herbe (The Future Generals)',
'Le Jeu de Balle (The Game of Balls)',
'Le Saut du Mouton (The Spring of Sheep)'.

A Touch of '8' for Debonair Roles

Spots of Leichner '5' and '9'
alternated round his face like warpaint
when we talked about my writing. 'One blockbuster
and you'll never have to work again,' he told me,
rubbing the red and white markings down to a tan
for drawing room comedy. He opened the window
onto an area where some old overcoats had been left
hanging on railings. 'Look at that!' he whispered,
'The Tramp's Cloakroom. Now there's a subject for you.'
We stared into the night. 'They'll be gone by October,'
he said, 'but where to, that's what we'll never know.'

A Start in Life

One such paragon, able to play anything from cuckolded
husbands to dainty blackmailers without his assumed character
being allowed to affect his performance in any way, was Hugh
Williams, at once heroic yet vulnerable. He watched me rehearse
my Dutch priest, then he came up to me and asked what I was
going to do in this scene. 'I don't know, Mr Williams,' I said,
adding hopefully, 'I thought I'd do nothing.'

'O no you don't,' he said, a trace of hardness entering his voice,
'I'm doing nothing in this scene.'

Peter Ustinov, *Dear Me*

Of course I wanted to be an actor. I had the gold chain
like Alain Delon. I could lift one eyebrow.
I didn't wear any socks.
I came home from France
with a brush-cut and a sketch of myself
and my father said 'WHAT ARE YOU GOING TO DO?'

[130]

Work had this mad glint in its eye
which made me look away.
I practised my draw in the mirror.
'The honeymoon's over,' said my father.
'I don't care what you do
so long as it isn't a politician, a poof, or a tenor.'

I made a face, scanning the South Downs
for something easier.
On a good day I could see the Chanctonbury Ring
outlined against the horizon.
'I want to be an actor,' I said.
My father slapped his knee.

'No you don't,' he shouted. 'You don't give a damn
about the theatre, or me. You write poetry.
When I was your age I'd seen every play in London.
I wanted passionately to act.
Can you say that?' His widow's peak
was like a judge's black cap as he laid down the law.

'Acting's showing off,' I said to the Downs.
'It's the perfect cover for people like us
who can't do anything else.
It's better than nothing anyway.'
I walked in the garden, shaking one of his collars
till it fell to pieces in my hand.

I dried my eyes, but I never did land
the job he was looking for. I stayed where I was,
waiting for a last call to find me
putting on make-up in my dressing-room –
'Five minutes please, Mr Williams' –
as if I could still go on

and make a start in life. I see the Downs even now
like a backdrop to the scene.
I put on different clothes and I see myself in action.
It feels like drawing a gun in slow motion
over and over again. I have the gold chain
like Alain Delon. I can lift one eyebrow.

Death of an Actor

i.m. Hugh Williams 1904–1969

1

Now that I am cold
Now that I look like him
I put on this warm grey suit of wool
In sympathy with my father.

Now that I'm alone
Now that I have come to this nice
Indifference
I sweep my hair straight back
The way he wore it during his life
And after he was dead
His fierce forehead
Still doubting the intelligence
Of those who approached where he lay.

2

Now that he is dead
Now that he is remembered
Unfavourably by some
For phrases too well cut

To fit their bonhomie
I wonder what he was like
This stiff theatrical man
With his air of sealed regret.
'I'd have made a first class tramp,'
He told me once,
'If I'd had more money.'

Now that it is late
Now that it is too late
For filial piety
I can but thank him for
His bloody-mindedness.
Face expressionless with pain
He ordered me a suit in Savile Row
The very day he took
The last plunge backwards
Into secrecy and sweat.
'O Dad, can dead men swim?'

3

Gold on the doorstep, whose steps
Nag the sand-drifts.
Gold in the spittoon.

My father would sit on the steps
Emptying his shoe.
Pitchers of sand on each step.

If they went on, they would lead
Back to my room. Gold in a silver spoon.
My father's throat torn to sand.

4

Our first Christmas after the war
A triangular package
Arrived from his producer.

'Greetings from Emile Littler'
Said the message printed on the bar
Of a single coathanger.

5

Now that I have tucked myself in
To this deep basement calm
And the windows are sealed for winter,
Now that my life is organized
To absorb the shock
Of looking back at it,
I understand why he put such vast whiskies
Into the hands of his enemies
And I take back what I said.

Now that I am grown
Now I have children of my own
To offer me their own
Disappointed obedience
I feel for him.
Our children left us both
Because we sat so still
And were too wise for them
When they told us their best jokes.

6

My father was last to leave the stage
In *The Cherry Orchard* in 1966.
He said to his bookshelves,
'My friends, my dear good friends,
How can I be silent?
How can I refrain from expressing, as I leave,
The thoughts that overwhelm my being?'
His sister was calling him,
'The station ... the train. Uncle,
Shouldn't we be going?'

7

The recording starts too late
To drown the sound of wheels. A little screen
Jerks upwards and the coffin
Wobbles towards us on rollers, like a diving board.
This is my father's curtain call. His white-ringed eyes
Flicker to the gallery as he bows to us. He bows
To his leading lady, then steps back again,
Rejoining hands with the cast.

In the dressing-room afterwards
He pours us all champagne:
'It's like a madhouse here. We're staffed by chumps.
The stage manager thinks the entire production
Stems from his control panel, like a cremation.
He's never heard of laughs. As for the set,
Tom says it's the old Jermyn Street Turkish Baths
Painted shit. Let's hope it doesn't run.'

8

Now that he is gone
Now that we have followed him this far
To a push-button crematorium
In unknown Golders Green
I think how near he seems, compared to formerly,
His head thrown back like that
Almost in laughter.
I used to watch him making up
In an underground dressing-room,
His head thrown back that way:
A cream and then a bright red spot
Rubbed down to a healthy tan.

Now that he is gone
Now that we have seen his coffin
Roll through those foul flaps
And a curtain ring down for the last time
On a sizeable man
I remember how calm he remained
Throughout the final scene,
Sitting bolt upright
On a windswept platform.
'The coldest place in the south of England,'
He used to say – off on tour again
In one of his own plays.

9

Now that he has returned to that station
Where the leave-train is waiting
Blacked-out and freezing,
The smell of whisky lingers on my breath,

A patch of blue sky
Stings like a slap in the face.

Now that he isn't coming down
On the midnight train tonight, or any night,
I realize how far
Death takes men on from where they were
And yet how soon
It brings them back again.

10

Now that I'm the same age
As he was during the war,
Now that I hold him up like a mirror
To look over my shoulder,
I'm given to wondering
What manner of man it was
Who walked in on us that day
In his final uniform.
A soldier with two families?
An actor without a career?
'You didn't know who on earth I was,' he told me.
'You just burst into tears.'

Now that he has walked out again
Leaving me no wiser,
Now that I'm sitting here like an actor
Waiting to go on,
I wish I could see again
That rude, forgiving man from World War II
And hear him goading me.
Dawdling in peacetime,
Not having to fight in my lifetime, left alone

To write poetry on the dole and be happy,
I'm given to wondering
What manner of man I might be.

Another Shot

When he falls asleep tonight, I'll sit still
with the stuffed crocodile, wondering what to do.
Have another shot from the bottle?
Or go upstairs and look for evidence of myself?
I've seen it all before – the toilet case
of film-star cigarette cards, the bundles of old
theatre programmes, unfinished albums
from Eden Roc and The Garden of Allah.
My father's elevators perish in a drawer.
His false beard weeps to itself.
Only his autograph, scrawled impatiently
on hundreds of pin-up photographs,
looks anything like mine, so patiently copied from it.
When I burst in on his sleep
with a head hollowed out of a turnip
swinging from a broom, the villain Steerforth
smiles at my innocence, Mr Darcy looks at me
through his eyeglass and asks if I've been drinking.

Speech Day
to Neil Rennie

It comes at you out of nowhere, with 'Hello, Muggins!
You still here?' or 'Myers was travelling through
Europe on his way to Strasbourg,' the sense of time
unravelling without you, the possibilities
of what might happen if you did nothing
running neck and neck with your attention span
in a sack race for the dead. It's too like life:
unwarranted enthusiasm somehow using itself up
in time for the end to happen, as when, on Speech Day,
the Head Boy comes to the front of the stage
to thank the staff for making it all possible
and us for bearing with him, in spite of the seating.

A Picture of a Girl in a Bikini

I look over the banisters and see, far down,
Miss Pyke taking Assembly. I push my feet
into a pair of Cambridge house shoes
half my size and shuffle downstairs.
When I answer my name there is a long silence,
then Miss Pyke asks me where I've been.
I tell her I was reading a book
and didn't notice the time.

I see I have a smaller desk this term
as a punishment for being late.
I have to sit sideways, facing Armitage,
who eats little pieces of blotting paper
dipped in ink. When the bell goes

I barge off down Lower Corridor
with my head down and my elbows out,
knocking everyone flying.

Hurrah! There's a letter for me today.
I'd rather have a parcel, but I'm always happy
when I see the familiar blue envelope
propped on the mantelpiece
on the other side of School Hall.
I don't open it straight away, of course.
I shove it in my pocket
and read it later, like a man.

I'm standing outside the Headmaster's Study
waiting for the green light to come on.
Either I've failed Common Entrance
or my parents have died. When I go in
he's sitting at his desk, staring out of the window.
For a long time we watch Sgt Burrows
pushing his marker round Long Field,
Mr Harvey taking fielding practice.

The Headmaster pulls his writing case towards him
and opens it with his paper knife.
Inside is the worst news in the world,
my copy of *Health & Efficiency* with a picture of a girl
in a bikini playing with a beach ball.
I must have left it under my mattress.
The Headmaster looks at me in disbelief
and asks, 'What is the meaning of this?'

A Collection of Literature

My Dear Williams,
I am sorry to have to bother you on this score,
but I feel it is my duty to let you know
what has come to light today. Under separate cover
I am sending you a collection of literature
which I have taken from Hugo.

This morning he left under his mattress
a copy of Health & Efficiency. *When taxed with this,*
he said he had bought it on Boxmoor Station
on his day out. He admitted that he had passed it on
to several other boys and during the course
of investigations it transpired
that he had a lot of other magazines of this type,
which he says he brought from home.

At first I thought it might have been a piece of
childish stupidity on his part,
but when all these other magazines came to light
I realized that it went deeper.

I am very surprised that Hugo, a boy of nearly eleven,
should be interested in this sort of thing.
I have had a long talk to him and tried to point out
some of the dangers into which he is running.
I hope I have convinced him,
but the matter will need careful watching
and so I am sure you will keep your eyes open
at home, just as I shall here.

Yours sincerely, Ralph Huband.

No Particular Place to Go

O'Sullivan's Record Exchange
in the Peskett Street Market
was out of bounds to Lower Boys
on account of Miss O'Sullivan's taste
in music. We used to jive
in the listening booths
when she turned the volume up for us,
knowing we wouldn't buy.
It was the best she could do.
You couldn't hear that kind of thing
any other way in 1956. The overloaded wires
must have set fire to the partitioning.
They had to throw hundreds of
twisted 78s out onto the pavement.

O'Sullivan's Record Exchange,
its record-covered walls suspended
in their own flames, still seems to welcome me
with all my favourite tunes,
and Miss O'Sullivan
moving her arms over the turntables
like one who heals. When I'm caught
loitering in the new car park
off Peskett Street ten years from now
and taken for questioning, I'll know
what to expect: 'Look here old boy,
the past is out of bounds, you should know that.'
'But sir,' I'll say, 'where else is there to go
on these half-holidays?'

Returning Soldier

He must be standing by a window, looking out
on a backdrop of Regent's Park. The sound
of carriage wheels on gravel, a woman's laugh.
As the lights come up, he moves to centre stage
to check his tie: the perfect kid-gloved cad.

In a government-issue busman's overcoat,
long in the sleeve,
a white arm-band for 'officer material',
he looks more like the wronged husband of the piece.
'Don't just do something, sit there'
was the word of command
to the men guarding Staines Railway Bridge
during the Phoney War.

As the dust settled I could see your father
stretched out beside the road, clutching a map.
I lifted him up
and propped him against the side of the jeep.
'Come on, sir,' I said. 'Have a cigarette, sir.
You always have a cigarette when you wake up.'
He didn't get the picture at first.
He thought he had trodden in something cold
and fallen over backwards.
'I got my bastard left foot wet,' he said.

Now that he's walking towards me in long shot,
limping a little from the war,
now that he pauses for a moment in close-up,
lighting a cigarette,
I find myself playing the kid-gloved cad

to his returning soldier.
I'm sitting on the edge of my seat
to find out what I say.

Going Round Afterwards

His face was orange.
His widow's peak had been blacked in.
I knew it was him,
because he didn't speak.
'Congratulations!' I said.
'I didn't know you could cry.'
His dresser was holding
a pair of check trousers
underneath his chin. He let the legs
drop through a coathanger
and smiled at me deafly.
'It's just a trick,' said my father.
'Anyone can do it.'
I stood there with my drink,
feeling the ingenious glamour
of being cramped, the mild delinquency
of things behind curtains –
shirts and cardigans
that should have been at home.
Did I have the guts?
And did you have to want it all that much
in order to go on?
His face came up from the wash basin
white and unwell again,
a trace of make-up underneath his ears.

His dresser was preparing
another pair of trousers,
holding them up off the floor
as my father stepped into them.

Now That I Hear Trains

Now that I hear trains
whistling out of Paddington on their way to Wales,
I like to think of him, as young as he was then,
running behind me along the sand,
holding my saddle steady
and launching me off on my own.

Now that I look unlike
the boy on the brand new bike
who wobbled away down the beach,
I hear him telling me: 'Keep pedalling, keep pedalling.'
When I looked over my shoulder
he was nowhere to be seen.

SELF-PORTRAIT WITH A SLIDE

(1990)

When I Grow Up

When I grow up I want to have a bad leg.
I want to limp down the street I live in
without knowing where I am. I want the disease
where you put your hand on your hip
and lean forward slightly, groaning to yourself.

If a little boy asks me the way
I'll try and touch him between the legs.
What a dirty old man I'm going to be when I grow up!
What shall we do with me?

I promise I'll be good
if you let me fall over in the street
and lie there calling like a baby bird. Please,
nobody come. I'm perfectly all right. I like it here.

I wonder would it be possible
to get me into a National Health Hospice
somewhere in Manchester?
I'll stand in the middle of my cubicle
holding onto a piece of string for safety,
shaking like a leaf at the thought of my suitcase.

I'd certainly like to have a nervous tic
so I can purse my lips up all the time
like Cecil Beaton. Can I be completely bald, please?
I love the smell of old pee.
Why can't I smell like that?

When I grow up I want a thin piece of steel
inserted into my penis for some reason.
Nobody's to tell me why it's there. I want to guess!
Tell me, is that a bottle of old Burgundy

under my bed? I never can tell
if I feel randy any more, can you?

I think it's only fair that I should be allowed
to cough up a bit of blood when I feel like it.
My daughter will bring me a special air cushion
to hold me upright and I'll watch
in baffled admiration as she blows it up for me.

Here's my list: nappies, story books, munchies,
something else. What was the other thing?
I can't remember exactly,
but when I grow up I'll know. When I grow up
I'll pluck at my bedclothes to collect lost thoughts.
I'll roll them into balls and swallow them.

Self-Portrait with a Speedboat

You wouldn't think it to look at me,
but I was a hot property once upon a time
to my sponsors, Johnson and Johnson Baby Oil.

I reached the final of the 1980
World Powerboat Championship – myself,
Lucy Manners, Werner Panic and the rest.

I was going for the record
of no hours, no minutes, no seconds
and I reckoned I was in with a chance.

I was dancing the *Self-Portrait* along
inside the yellow buoys, nice dry water ahead,
when I started picking up some nonsense

from my old rival Renato Salvadori,
the knitwear salesman from Lake Como,
appearing for Martini.

Renato was chopping up the water with a series
of kick turns and yells and throwing it
in my face like a gauntlet, flak

from his tailplane running off my goggles.
I was pushing the *Self-Portrait*
into a sizeable swell, but I figured the aerofoil

would keep her nose down in an emergency,
the head-rest would account for any recoil
occasioned by overdrive – 4g,

that's about four times your body weight
screwing your neck around on corners
and pinning a smile on your face.

I looked over my shoulder and saw Werner Panic
hovering and bouncing about.
The three of us hit the Guinness hairpin

at about ninety, sashaying our arses
round the corner post and spraying the customers
with soda water, which they didn't seem to mind.

You can either go into these things tight
and come out wide, or you can go in wide
and come out tight, depending on your mood.

But whereas Werner and myself went into it
tight and came out of it laughing,
Renato lost his bottle completely

and wound up pointing backwards in a pool
of engine oil, miming outrage
and holding out his hands to the judges.

His departure for Lake Como in the relief launch,
clutching his crash helmet
and lucky sombrero mascot,

left me aqua-planing the wash
from Werner's dogleg, covert blue and gold
tobacco logo making me see red.

I'm very fond of Werner, but I'm not about to
hand him the trophy on a platter
just because he smokes Rothmans.

I sat on his coat-tails for a lap or two,
revs going from 7½ to ten thou,
big V8 engine powering along at about a hundred.

I'll never forget his face
as the *Self-Portrait* took off on his starboard wake
and entered the unofficial record books

for ski-jumping – 19 feet of aluminium
chucked in a great curve between heaven and earth –
a trajectory to nowhere as it turned out,

but I didn't know that then. As I looked down
on the scene spread out beneath me,
I remember thinking what a fabulous

powerboat atmosphere there was
on the Royal Docks that afternoon –
champagne and cigars, jellied eels, a Big Top

with four shows a day, dolphins, a gorilla,
girls in pink leotards, all the fun of the fair.
As I touched down near the pits

my arm came up to say 'thank-you' to my mechanics
for making it all possible.
You can see one of them – Pasquale, that is –

returning the compliment at the exact moment
the *Self-Portrait* hits the pier
of the escape basin and vanishes under a layer

of polystyrene blocks, old aerosol cans
and water-logged flyers for the 1980
World Powerboat Championship. That's me

standing up to my neck in dirty water,
holding up a shattered steering-wheel
to cheers from the salvage barge.

On the Road

A boy came through a door in Opelousas
and stuck two fingers in the air
at a car that was going past
carrying a tourist with nothing better to do
than write down everything he saw
as he travelled around America –
Franklin's Skating Arena and Shoe Repair,
End Of The World Sale Of Night Crawlers, dogs
mating in a town called Gun Barrel, Texas,
a boy who stuck two fingers in the air
and went back through a door in Opelousas.

Dumb Show

The would-be bride is here,
blindfold against the setting sun.
Her heart-shaped bag
has been eaten by her fiancé, the alsatian.
She is armed and smiling
as she stumbles among us with a curse.

Lighting a Greek candle, she curtsies wrongly
and ascends a ladder
let down by one of her assailants.
'Everyone wants to be me!' she cries,
as she dives out of the window
into a barrel of laughs.

Sex

'Sex' seems to be a word that most people understand,
so there is a fair chance that the woman will understand
what the man is getting at when he mentions the subject.

Perhaps he is finding difficulty getting into the passage
and it may be necessary to ask why. Perhaps she is dry
because there is no natural lubricant for the penis,

or perhaps she is very tense and unable to accept him.
It may be that the fault lies with the man, if he cannot
complete the sexual act, or his climax comes too soon.

At this point it may be necessary to enquire about
    orgasm.
As sexual excitement reaches its climax (orgasm), the
    man
will recognize that the jerking out of his semen
    (sperm)

is about to start and that it is inevitable. His semen
is said to be 'coming' and if any discussion is needed
the verb 'to come' may be used without causing
    offence.

For instance, the woman may be asked if she
    understands
what the word 'coming' means in this context
and whether she has ever experienced such a thing.

Does she feel herself to be on the verge of 'coming',
only to find herself drawing back from it because of
    some
unspecified mental problem, and if so, what?

The World of Work

At six the cup of tea is set down.
How the cup of tea is set down.
Quietly, or with suppressed fury.
Jim looks at the face of his wife sleeping
and decides to be horrible.
The bathroom was cold.
He forgot to put on the fire.

He crosses to the window in a rage
and draws the curtains back.
How the curtains are drawn back.
Gently but firmly?
Or practically ripped from their hooks?
Jim thinks her room is too hot
and throws the window up.

She wakes in panic, sitting up in bed.
'Where am I? What am I doing here?'
(She has on her scarf.)
'It's only me, dear. Time to go to work.
Me of course, not you.'
She makes her noise. 'For God's sake
come home with something interesting tonight.'

Jim crawls to his place of employment
and sinks down exhausted at his drill.
What can she possibly have meant?
She's seen the rubber aprons and sheets,
protective floor coverings
and face-guards from Asbestos,
machine maintenance slack.

He's taken her lubricated gloves,
heavy duty cooling agents from Cosmetics,
bone meal from Catering.
What more could she desire?
An industrial caution perhaps?
A concrete overcoat? 'Oh yes,
love needs funding,' he reflects sadly.

After work Jim steals a disused
tarpaulin from Bulk Haulage,
a bottle of turps from Ancillary Staff,

a cast-iron alibi from Personnel.
He's going to forgive his wife this time
if it's the last thing he does.
He can hardly wait to get home.

How the table will look
laid with the soiled tarpaulin.
How the glasses will shine
brimming with tomorrow's tears.
'Oh yes, love needs funding, dear,' he remarks,
imagining some in-home gratitude
on the stolen Axminster.

He's out of luck. Mrs Jim
takes hold of the tarpaulin in her teeth
and runs out into the road.
How the turpentine drains into Jim's old
factory work boots and socks.
How Jim rewinds the alarm clock
for another working day.

The Spell

Now you are far away, it is as if you slept
beside me here again and I watched over you,
    remembering
the spell I had tried not to break by waking you.
As I watched you sleep, it seemed I had only to reach out
and touch you for you to wake at last in my arms.

Self-Portrait with a Map of Ireland

1

The nurses are asleep
on 'A' and 'B' corridors
as I take the bin-liners from their frames,
tie knots in them
and sling them down the chute
into the garbage skip.
A broken milk bottle
has torn a hole in one of the bags.
Sour milk leaks out on my overalls.

Eight thirty. Here and there in the distance
alarms go off,
the sound of bedsprings complaining softly
under their shifting load.
A cardboard sign
with a moveable clock-hand in the shape of a leg
hangs outside Nurse Bluebell's room,
informing the world
of exactly what she is doing
at any hour of the day.
With the hand on 'Asleep'
she is urging her lover to come quickly now
or she'll be late for work.
I hold my breath and wait.

2

In the Staff Room, Mr Arnold,
my immediate superior
at England's Lane Nurses' Hostel,

is reading page 3 of *The Sun*.
He thinks it's disgusting
the way nurses invite men up to their rooms
then expect staff
to replace their beds for them.
'They aren't built to withstand that sort of
behaviour. If they want a bunk-up
they should do it in the car park like the rest.'
He turns their thermostat way down
and keeps them short of toilet paper
so they have to ask him for it
over and over again.

3

Nine fifteen. Men and boys
are quitting England's Lane by every exit.
Sandra Lewis walks slightly ahead
of her latest conquest, the anaesthetist.
They wait for the lift that never comes.
Through a half-open door
I see Dolores Fenton pinning up her hair.
Outside her room a joke thermometer
indicates 'Late Shift'.
A poster of the moon warns visitors,
'Heaven and Earth Shall Pass Away.
But My Words Shall Not Pass Away.'
We haven't spoken yet.

My job for today
is cleaning out the hood
of the ancient Aga
in the hostel refectory. I want Dolores Fenton
to see me performing this disgusting task

with a good grace
when she comes down to breakfast.
To make her laugh
I am wearing a hard hat and mask.

I lend her my *Daily Express*
and she asks me to replace her overhead bulb for her
without going through the Office.
Luckily it is my week
to hold the key to the Dispensary,
so I get her two 100-watt bulbs
instead of the usual 60-watt one,
a bag of mothballs
and a box of Lifebuoy soap.

No one answers when I knock on her door
so I let myself in and have a look around.
Cups for gymnastics line the shelf.
Pictures of badgers and otters
crowd round the narrow bed. In the bedside table
a packet of Durex Nu-Form
takes me by surprise.
When she comes through the door
I am standing on a chair, fixing the bulb for her.
She checks the switch.
Smiles come on all round.

4

This afternoon, Sister Beamish and I
are touring the corridors
on our monthly 'fact-finding mission'.
She knows where to look
for the tell-tale 'map of Ireland'

printed on a sheet,
the different-coloured hair
on hairbrush or comb,
the bristles round the brim of a washbasin.
She sniffs the air like a gun-dog,
scenting the elusive male of the species.

We have come to the room
with a cardboard thermometer hanging outside
and a poster of the moon.
Ma Beamish flings open the door
and switches on the light.
I stand to one side,
holding my clipboard and pen,
while Dolores Fenton's boyfriend
struggles into his clothes.

5

We take our break
and retire to the Office
for tea and Garibaldis from a special tin
depicting the Queen and Duke of Edinburgh
rock 'n' rolling.
Ma Beamish remembers a day
when the Royal Free Nurses' Hostel
was a decent, moral place
and she herself was still young.

'Sister Peele would welcome new arrivals
from Ireland and The North
with a talk in the Smoking Room:
"No men above stairs
under any pretext whatever. If you get the urge

[161]

you can always bring yourselves off." '
Ma Beamish dunks another Garibaldi in her tea
and shakes her head
'We should put a red light up over the door
and call it The Royal Free and Easy.'

6

Now the girls are coming home
blood-stained and tired from Early Shift,
checking their pigeon holes
and making calls.
'No letter again today. What's got into him?'
The showers come on upstairs,
soap bubbles foam from the waste outlet
where I am trying to unblock the grating
with a piece of wire.
Dirty water spreads out over the yard.

I say it's leaves falling on the roof
that are causing the trouble,
but Mr Arnold insists
it's the used contraceptives
the young doctors fling out of the windows
on Junior Corridor.
He finds a long pink one in the gutter
and holds it up to the light like a connoisseur.
'I wonder where this little baby's been?'
Then he drapes it across the windscreen
of somebody's car: his personal parking ticket.

The Junior

Elaine hates touching the heads
of the older women in Giovanni's.
She has to cope with styles
that are hardly more than a few strands
clinging to bone.
She feels desperate
until the smell of poor cooking
is drowned by the detergent.
Elaine, 17, is pregnant, but by whom?
She was doing Ruby's hair today
when it started to come away on the comb
exactly like her mother's.
'It wasn't me,' she wanted to say
when the manageress shouted at her
for spilling the dye, but the whole shop
thought how lovely Ruby's hair looked
when it came out coloured pink.
'Who's the lucky fella?' asked Ruby's husband,
putting his head round the door.
But he knew it had to be him.

Now the scissors are laid aside
and the lampshades relieved
of all the pimp-work they have to do
on behalf of the mirrors.
The reptilian manageress
puts on the strip lighting with a frown
and switches out the sign.
Elaine, being junior, has to clear.
She feels dead, but there's nowhere to go
in this shallow lock-up

to escape the stares from the street.
She sweeps the day's clippings
into a corner, remembering a time
when she wanted to work her way up
in Giovanni's, as a colour artist.
She picks up a handful of the hair
and looks at it for a moment.
Then she throws it back on the floor.
She must hurry now
if she doesn't want Simon to see her.

Wow and Flutter

The girl in O'Sullivan's Record Exchange
tips another lousy blues compilation
out of its worn-out inner sleeve
and holds it up to the light for my inspection.
'All right dear?'

Like the back of my head
in the barber's fluttering hand-mirror,
this looks like another one for my collection
that is going to be 'Absolutely great, thanks' –
until I get it home.

Desk Duty

My desk has brought me
all my worst fears on a big tray
and left it across my lap.

I'm not allowed to move until I have
eaten everything up.
I push things around on my plate.
I kick the heating pipes.

A piece of worn carpet on the floor
proves how long I've been sitting here
shuffling my feet,
opening and closing drawers,
looking for something I've lost
under piles of official papers and threats,
roofing grants and housing benefits.

Am I married or single?
Employed or self-employed?
What sort of work do I do?
Is my house being used for business
or entertainment purposes? (See Note 3)
If I am resident at my place of work,
who supplies the furniture?

I have cause to suspect myself
of deliberately wasting time
writing my name and place of birth
under 'Who else lives with you?'
It has taken me all day
to find something true to write
under 'Personal Allowances' – or not untrue.

I know all about my little game
of declaring more than I earn
to the Inland Revenue – or was it less?
I'm guilty as hell,
or I wouldn't be sitting here like this

playing footy-footy with my desk.
I'd be upstairs in bed with my bed.

Sonny Jim's House

The cistern groans under a new pressure.
Little-known taps are being turned on
in obscure regions of the house,
cutting off the water for his tea.
Jim forwards her mail to the garden, laughing
because he has hidden the marmalade.

At nine they both stay home and do nothing,
out of work. The ring in the bath and the
hacked loaf prove he is on the track
of his elusive wife. Her movements displace
the usual volume of elegant soft porn: face-
creams and cigarettes. Now Jim has razor-burn.

By the end of the afternoon he will have taken
a dozen pairs of sex-oriented shoes
back to her dressing-room. Jim swears
he can still see the funny side of life
in a halfway house where even the shoes
exist in limbo and the handrail is loose.

He puts his ear to the door of the study,
rushes in, sees the back of his head.
This is where he sits alone, in coffee-shock,
making lists of women. Photos of his wife
line the walls, reminding him of her.
The cupboard is open. He can't decide what to wear.

When the front door bangs he imagines his wife
has gone out and runs upstairs to look at
her clothes. Blocked by her breakfast tray,
he comes back down again, asking himself
whether the hall is part of the original house
or something to do with the street.

Jim thinks there are two houses here,
each one overlapping the other, like towels,
the spiral stair acting as a kind of hinge
for correct and incorrect behaviour. He stands
for hours on end, rolling his eyes
in soapy water dreams, unable to go up or down.

Lightly Clenched Fists

Steam clears from the shaving mirror
and a view of eternity presents itself.
The sensation of falling reminds me of my desk.
I wonder what it would be like
if you were walking along
and suddenly you liked Karlheinz Stockhausen.
Bad writing is so like good writing,
don't you think? But never quite enough.
The open notebook which looks like a girl's bottom,
the jet of warm water directed at your trousers,
foam coming up through the plughole for some reason.
The quiet period on my own with a good book
goes floating past on a lilo in the sun.
The visit to the farm appears on the horizon
where everything remains to be seen.

World's End

to Neil Rennie

Jim returns to his favourite Carnaby St boutique
circa 1966 and nods his shaggy head.
'Hi, Barry! Hi, Stu! Got the new flares in yet?'
The two Goths behind the counter in Plastic Passion
have heard about people like Jim. One of them
looks out a pair of tangerine elephant loons
left over from his father's 'Chocolate Taxi' scene
and throws them to Jim as a joke. The mildewed
    hipsters
have purple paisley inserts, patch pockets, studs
and novelty exterior fly-buttons with cannabis leaves.
Jim's eyes shine to see the switched-on funky gear.
He lies down on his back to get into them.

It is Saturday afternoon, as usual in Jim's life.
He wants to show off his new maxi-loons, 3-storey
snakeskin platforms and Mr Freedom T-shirt
with the half-peeled banana batiked on the front
to the in-crowd at the Chelsea Drugstore, demolished
in 1974. He dons his freaky leather hat and shades
and sets off down the King's Road at a leisurely
mile a year, his flares trailing a year or two behind.
By the time they catch up with him, wrapping
    themselves
gradually round his spindly legs like sails,
the King's Road is deserted. The street lamps don't
    work.
Jim strikes a match. It looks like World's End.

In the Seventies

It shouldn't be such a bad day. Tony and I
are delivering copies of *The New Review*
to newsagents in north London.
One of us drives the van, while the other
dashes inside with the invoice book.

Most of the shops in this area
have been taken over by Ugandan Asians
who sit under canopies of soft porn
wobbling their heads at us: 'As you see,
we have so little room for display purposes ...'

Judging from the miles of overlapping
buttocks and tits, this month's position
is down on all fours in 'the den',
the woman's face crushed in a tiger skin.
'Forgive me, sir,' says the manager,

flicking the pages of our fine but
slow-moving publication. 'This sort of thing ...'
He pauses for a moment at 'In Between the Sheets'
by Ian McEwan. 'If we are honest,
it only hangs around collecting dust ...'

Them

How perfect they are without our help,
these limited editions. How even in winter
they seem to shine when you see them,
marching ahead of you, dead set on something.

Their breasts toss things to porters, who bow.
Their knees touch as they get down into cars.
They look so interesting in their savage furs
you can't imagine their parents or their homes
or whether their beds have turndowns.

Do they sleep, these dreams? It seems impossible
that they go willingly into darkened rooms with men,
there to make love with nothing on,
when they could be walking about in the open.

Here comes one now. Can you stop from reading on?
Her heels are bound in such sweet leather.
Her hair has been cut by God, regardless of the fashion.

She knows you are following her,
for she tilts you this way and that in the sun,
catching a glimpse of herself in a new hat
as she turns down Regent Street.

Did she go into Dickins and Jones?
You followed her, but she had left by the other door.
You ran out, but already she was getting into a car
when the man with a little boy came up
and asked you the way to Carnaby Street.

Sonny Jim Alone

There aren't enough sockets in Jim's room
to accommodate his troubled thoughts.
He runs downstairs in his track suit
and scores a two-way adaptor

from the communal kitchen,
a rubber band from Administration.

Now the hoover and electric toothbrush
spring to life in his hands.
He can almost imagine Cheryl from Hammersmith
here in the room with him,
but the flex from the toothbrush
won't reach as far as the sofa.

Red-headed Cheryl is overjoyed
to have found a position looking after dolphins
so soon after leaving school.
Blonde Elaine, junior colour artist
at Giovanni's Hair Salon,
has a walk-on part as a waitress
in *Bush Babies* with Roger Moore.

Tantalizing Tina from Tonbridge
has got it all figured out.
She used to be an accountant
with a firm of market researchers in cosmetics,
until she put two and two together
and came up with herself.

Jim reads the folded newspaper
over and over again, his lips moving,
his eyes popping out of his head.
His collection of hairstyles and limbs,
assembled over the years
from *Weight Watchers' Weekly* and *Time Out*,
are laid on the sofa under the Anglepoise.
(His favourite has a tyre mark across her mouth.)

As he runs around eating a Mars
and checking the angles of vision
from the houses opposite, a dozen pairs of eyes
seem to follow him round the room.
Supposing someone came in? What would he say?
Where would he put everything?

One Pilot, One Crew

You're walking home late at night after a party.
It sounds like a possible first line
and you write it down in your address book.

On the opposite page a girl's name stands out,
Ari-Non or Nori-An, the names of one or two
Malay nurses you remember meeting,

or that of the Malay airline pilot
who took you, as far as you remember, in his car.
You're wondering where to go from there

when you fancy the figure of a nurse
keeping pace on the opposite side of the street,
Nori-An or Ari-Non, stopping when you stop,

or bending to tie her shoe. You try the line
'How about making us both some coffee?'
But the nurse has heard that somewhere before.

'No milk, no coffee,' she replies.
'You've got some water, haven't you?'
'Sure. You want glassawatter?' She has opened a door

on the usual bed-sitting room
where two double beds have been pushed together
and two Malay boys lie asleep in one another's arms.

'Whose idea are they?' you ask, pointing to the boys.
'I dunno,' says the nurse. 'One pilot, one crew.
Wassamatter, don't you like Malay?'

Couples in Love

Couples in love cock their heads about
and make small, peculiar facial movements
as they gaze into one another's eyes.
Their facial muscles become taut,
their skin becomes flushed or pale,
their eyes become clearer or brighter.

Other minuscule changes take place
within the eye itself, a fact recognized
by oriental jade dealers,
who veil their eyes during bargaining
to hide their excitement
and avoid any increase in the asking price.

Daffodils

I remember drawing back the curtains
and seeing my neighbour Georgie Windows
for the first time.
He was standing on the window sill,
polishing the air of our open window

in four-four time. I didn't realize then
that he was the happy genius of our street.
He worked at first-floor level.
While his wife went along
knocking on front doors, Georgie made himself known
to the couples upstairs in bed.
He'd been wondering, he said,
whether there was anyone living here any more,
or whether we were hibernating.

He used to take his motorbike to Wales
at about this time of year.
We always knew it was Spring
when Georgie swore in Welsh
and took off into the blue, his eternal
wife strapped to his back,
his ladder to heaven.
He came home early this time last year,
having left her alone there.
He'd ridden all night and made it home
in record time, just in time to go to work.
She was waiting on the doorstep for him,
the house all clean and welcoming,
his favourite daffodils in every room.

Jim's Dance

Now Jim lives in squalor with his former wife,
or thinks he does. He never sees her any more,
unless she is furious, or pregnant,
and even then she uses her hand as a veil
when they pass one another in the hall.

Jim doesn't mind. He thinks of these meetings
as the steps of a dance he's learning,
where everyone closes their eyes for a moment
as they come forward to bow. He closes his eyes
and bows to her image on the stairs.

Jim's wife is hardly more than a word of command
to him now, a shopping-list pinned to his overalls.
He looks for her in the old nursery
and in the bar, knowing that if he catches her eye
it will be bad luck all day.

Voice Over

There comes a point in this song
when I hear your voice
calling my name outside the door
and for one moment
I think you are still here,
terror and desire competing
for my suddenly pounding heart.

Toilet

I wonder will I speak to the girl
sitting opposite me on this train.
I wonder will my mouth open and say,
'Are you going all the way
to Newcastle?' or 'Can I get you a coffee?'

Or will it simply go 'aaaaah'
as if it had a mind of its own?

Half closing eggshell blue eyes,
she runs her hand through her hair
so that it clings to the carriage cloth,
then slowly frees itself.
She finds a brush and her long fair hair
flies back and forth like an African fly-whisk,
making me feel dizzy.

Suddenly, without warning,
she packs it all away in a rubber band
because I have forgotten to look out
the window for a moment.
A coffee is granted permission
to pass between her lips
and does so eagerly, without fuss.

A tunnel finds us looking out the window
into one another's eyes. She leaves her seat,
but I know that she likes me
because the light saying 'TOILET'
has come on, a sign that she is lifting
her skirt, taking down her pants
and peeing all over my face.

Creative Writing

Trying to persuade about fifteen
Creative Writing students (Poetry)
to put more images into their work,
I was fiddling in my pocket

with an old contraceptive packet,
put there at the start of the course
and long since forgotten about.

If you don't mind my saying so
you seem to see everything
from the man's point of view
exactly like my husband.
What happened to women's poetry
in the last two thousand years?
What about Sappho?
What about Sharon Olds?

The foil wrapper of the Durex Gossamer,
weakened by hours of friction,
gave way and my fingers found themselves
rubbing together in a mess
of spermicide and vaginal lubricant.

Day Return

Your work up north takes longer than you think.
You have to have a drink with a man
who doesn't have a home to go to
and lets his hand fall heavily on your own
in explanation. The train he finds for you
is a mockery of a train
and keeps slipping backwards into wartime obscurity –
blackouts and unexplained halts.

Is it really the same day
you arrived in that northern city in a clean shirt
and walked through sunfilled streets

with half an hour to kill?
You sit in your corner seat
holding your ticket in your hand.
Someone asks if there is a buffet car on the train
and is told he must be joking.

Jim Flips His Wig

The first white hair was the first
screw coming loose. He took no notice.
He smoothed it down with his brush.

Now a whole gang of little pubic horrors
is springing from his skull at all angles,
putting up their hands in class
to ask Jim what they're for.

Jim doesn't know. He cuts them short.
He thinks he'd look more intelligent and smart
without any hair at all, so he pulls it out
in handfuls and throws it away.

As he turns to admire his handiwork in the glass,
comic book mainsprings and bells
burst from his head like an overwound
alarm clock, bringing the house down.

See how his long dark hair
conceals a curly fright-wig underneath.
What a great idea to come as Harpo Marx!

Self-Portrait with a Spare Crash Helmet

'Are you a member, sir?'
Of course I'm not, so I have to pay in full
for the pleasure of entering some former gents
where even I can tell
fulfilment isn't waiting
in the smell of beer and men.

Is it worth it, cruising the streets for fun,
johnnies in your pocket,
a spare crash helmet slung on the handlebars?
If I don't slide under a bus in the rain,
the bike breaks down
or I'm stopped by the cops again.

My room is comfortable, warm and bright.
Why can't I stay in it and work?
When darkness falls, like some excuse from God,
I weaken inwardly, I melt
for little sighs and looks,
for words that don't make sense.

'Desire, desire ...' How does it go?
'I have too dearly bought ...'
When someone asks me for a light, I jump
six inches in the smoke-filled air
and come down with a bump. What am I doing here
in The Borderline at half past two?

The later it gets, the younger everyone looks,
the longer ago. The girls coming through the door
are probably children by now
dropping by on their way to school.

For what they are and for what they do ...
my body drags its feet.

When I see a cigarette in my hand
I know I must be drunk.
I watch a girl in underwear and lace
being drawn back and forth on a string
which runs from the ladies down a flickering stair
to the dance floor below.

She reels herself in across the dark pools of eyes
and back up the stairs again.
I feel the heat of her body on my face
as she passes in front of me.
I ask her to dance and she rolls enormous eyes
because I am so weird.

She points a little pointy finger at the stage
and brings it to her lips.
The music stops, paralysing my features.
Something called 'Jungle Boy'
is dragging its congos forward like a ball and chain.
I think I have not a right feeling towards women.

The Best in the World

You girls whose talk is all of Pop,
you're showing off to us
in your halter-tops and slacks.
Your looks announce with such mild cruelty
that this is all there is
and all there ever was
of happiness in Young America.

'It's the best-in-the-world!' you say
when you stand your boyfriends up
just to be here tonight,
revolving, alone, in the spotlight.
'Try it, you'll like it,' you say,
'It's the Real Thing.'
When you dance in close
you turn your backs for fun:
pop heels, pop curls, pop eye-shadow.
You know what's going on
is the best in the world for us.
(You don't say yes just yet,
but you're fixed up for sure.)
You lean towards us and say,
'Perfection would be ...'
You say 'Purr-fection' like the disc-jockey,
flicking back your hair.
You aren't around to tell us any more.
You're moving on in Young America.

Desire

Arching perfectly plucked eyebrows
over blue eggshell eyes
she tells me it is possible in her country
to go all the way
from Viipuri on the Gulf of Finland
to Jisalmi, far inland,
on little steamers
which thread through channels in the rocks
and forested islands.

Moving her hand through the air
she describes how certain rivers and lakes
cascade into other lakes
in magnificent waterfalls
which provide all the electricity for Finland.

Lost Lines

Even before you turned your head
you knew it was one of them –
neither woman nor man
but one of those images
that sweep through revolving doors
into thinner air,
leaving a draught where you stand,
a shiver down your spine.

Your life isn't long enough
to follow where they are going.
You will come to an end, die
and be forgotten about
and they will be tapping a little foot
on the other side of town,
where someone half turns their head,
knowing it is one of them.

The Trick

If only the trick were letting a record
spin over between your hands,

setting the needle down
and returning to your seat.

If only it could be done
by getting comfortable again,
your head leaning on your hand,
your eyelids drooping.

If only it would help in some way
to gather your papers in your hands
and bang them on the table-top
to get their edges aligned.

You could hold all your papers in one hand
and splay them out like a fan.
You could riffle through them occasionally,
as if you were looking for something.

When your papers fell from your hand
and scattered round your chair,
you could sit for hours on end
without so much as a move.

Everyone Knows This

Everyone knows this –
the tiny, insane voluptuousness
of writing a cheque, ticking it off
on a list, retiring to the sofa.
Something like a report or a letter
hangs over your head, books and magazines
pile up, free offers
of Kodachrome, conditioners, tea-bags,

holidays on Mount Everest.
You lay down your pen for a moment
and somehow or other
never pick it up again.
Your handkerchief falls out of reach.
You get to your feet, having accumulated
one nice and one nasty thing to do
and do the nice thing first.
You open the fridge door and stare for a while
into that little lighted world
with its air of hopefulness.
You'd like to go out, but it isn't raining yet.

Sonny Jim on Parade

If this is Jim, marching up and down
in his room, swinging his arms up and down
and drilling his men,
why do horse-hairs, curly-wurly things,
nothing like his own thoughts,
break free from the surrounding calm
and pop up like question marks
on the ends of his commands?
'Left wheel?' 'Right wheel?' 'Attention?'
Jim shakes his head from side to side,
as if to get rid of some irritating
chattering noise from the ranks.
'By the front. Quick march!'
Jim takes the salute with his comb.

The Offence

According to Jim, it all began innocently enough
in a wood near the caravan site where the two boys
had been holidaying with their grandparents.

Jim was practising with a punchball
when out of the bushes rushed the two brothers
wearing warpaint and feathers and uttering cries.

They persuaded Jim to take part in a game
of Cowboys and Indians, warning him
that he would be scalped if they took him alive.

He was duly captured and tied to a tall tree,
where we found him next morning, naked
and weeping and suffering from exposure.

His head had been shaved. His face and body
had been smeared with lipstick. He told us about it
in sign language and gibberish.

After carrying out extensive enquiries in the area
we could find no trace of these brothers,
their grandparents, or their holiday caravan.

In the lonely spot described to us by Jim
we found only his tent, a simple Wigwam type,
in which he had been living alone for several weeks

on tins of tuna fish. Among the few items left
lying about, we found various articles of make-up,
lipstick, a mirror, and a pair of hair-clippers.

Saint Jim

Jim sits in glory in his home-made chair,
one hand slightly raised, holding a ten pound note.
His face and moustache are smeared black.
His widow's peak is visible under the brim
of a stetson. Bunched at his throat,
a dozen gaudy ties, the gift of petitioners.

On the walls of the reception area, a Marlboro ad,
naked women, a plaque thanking Jim
for a miracle. 'If you visit, please make some
donation to my needs, or help with the cleaning.'
I hold his gloved hand in mine
and whisper how handsome he is looking.

He makes no reply. His eyes follow me round the room
as I light candles or scrape wax from the floor.
I tap ash from his cigarette and place it
in a polythene bag, for everything in the world
is Jim's and has to be put away.
He turns a page of *Playboy* magazine.

His bottle of gin he keeps in the Air France
flight-bag slung on the arm of his chair. It won't be long
till he is singing one of the songs from *Kismet*
or *Guys and Dolls*: 'If we only had a lousy little grand
we could be a millionaire.' Or complaining about the
     service
in this 'once great hotel'.

Self-Portrait with a Slide

Assembled with me on the long slide
are breakfast, lunch and tea,
their preparation and consumption by me
and the washing up afterwards
stacked and waiting in the sink.
I have to go down the slide, balancing a tray
both full and empty, hot and cold,
looking both hungry and satisfied,
bored, excited and tired. I stand at the top
in pyjamas and dressing-gown.
I mustn't forget my mat.

Mornings are dizzying, looking over the edge
at a stub of pencil
lying on the breakfast table.
I have been standing on the landing until now,
indicating my face
with a slack index finger,
not wanting to hurt myself going down.
The monitor taps me on the shoulder: time to go.
I rise to my toes
and throw off my dressing-gown.
I raise one hand in the air.
Pieces of coastline and sky are dragged across my sight
as I swerve to avoid the bathroom.
We're off, I suppose,
if a wave of homesickness is anything to go by.
I remember my bedroom with a sigh.

Now the long slope of the day
pitches forward slightly,
causing me to stumble.

Papers and books pile up behind my back,
anxious to pass me and get on.
Washing tangles my feet.
The sofa, the horse ride, the supermarket
nudge and buffet one another,
lurching to one side. I come out of a spiral
clinging to the handrail for my life.
I overtake my stereo, stuck in the last groove
of *Lift to the Scaffold*.

My eyes are cast down,
as if from modesty or embarrassment.
My half-closed hands
lie on the table in front of me
where I can see them. From the way I am sitting
staring at a sheet of paper,
something would seem to be the matter.
Perhaps I am ill?
Or the temperature of my pen won't come down?
I lean over myself
with a concerned expression on my face,
as if I am visiting.
I think of something kind to say.
How am I feeling today?
What would I like to eat?
My pen moves jerkily over the paper
for a moment, like the needle of an instrument
for recording brain-life.
From the other side of the street
I look like someone writing. My head comes up
as if I am pausing to think.

I've changed a lot in the last five minutes.
I'm not here most of the time.

I'm over here behind the door.
I'm willing to turn a blind eye
to some of the things I do,
but I like to know where I am
in case I have to go out.

It's sad to see me going so far away all alone,
but I have my permission to come back
whenever I like
and start again.
I can't remember where I was.
I forgot to mark my place.

Is the stub of pencil where I left it,
arrested in mid-flight?
If I lean out,
I can touch it with my finger as I pass.
I can't get hold of it. One false move
and it drifts out of reach
behind the breakfast tray, vibrating uselessly.
If I could nudge it into the upright position
I might feel able
to describe the kind of grip
that would hold it still for a moment
while I concentrate.
My eyelids droop
and I have a more interesting experience
for a few seconds, working in plasticine.

Now everything is slipping through my fingers
into the next-door room
where I am trying not to slide down to the kitchen
for a bite to eat.
I feel the wind brushing my face

[189]

as I shoot across the kitchen into the hall.
My hair flies out behind me,
making me look free,
but I am in the street, alas, wasting time shopping.
I dig in my heels
and my hair flies forward in my eyes. Dogs bark
as I peer into my house while I am out.

I thought I had found a way down
through the system of snacks and mood changes
that constitutes an average day
on the slide,
but I have lost my footing
in the loose hours before tea.
I veer from side to side.
I throw my tray in the air.
So much rubble has broken loose
since this morning began so promisingly
with a friendly push from behind
that I scramble on all fours
across an escarpment of coffee cups.
I cling to the tablecloth.

Is this The End coming up to meet me
waving excitedly? I reach out my hand
to touch the patch of sunlight or yellow lichen
on the bedroom window-sill –
shadowy patches of fungus,
or the yellow primer showing through?
It's hard to tell
when the pencil hovers in mid-air
leaving only a blur.
I thought I had reached ground level
and could shake the Champagne bottle

to a celebratory fizz,
but this looks like the start of something new.
The monitor gives me a push and down I go,
uttering involuntary cries.

Deserter

The days hang back. They come at me
in shock-waves, like bad news. They dawn so late
I sometimes think I missed one in my sleep
and lie here counting them. From where I lie
I can see them parading past my window
like soldiers going to war. White curtains
drawn back and forth across my sight
are handkerchiefs in the hands of girls
waving goodbye to their loved ones.

I see them coming round again,
accusing me with their blood-stained uniforms
of having betrayed them. Her body falls
like a too bright light on my surroundings.
Motes of dust, revolving in the first rays of sun
are all it takes to make me feel afraid.

Bath Night

A nurse kneels on the floor of the bath house
pulling loose Jim's protective underclothes.
'Washing you,' she murmurs,
touching the marks left by the laces.
'Remember now. Washing you.'

Jim stands up very straight and tall,
his eyes screwed shut.
His toes grip the edge of the bath mat.
'Washing you,' he repeats after her.
'Remember washing you.'

The nurse picks up Jim in her arms
and lets him slip out of the towel
into the disinfected water. His wasted legs
loom to the surface like slender birch trunks.
His feet stand up like pale stalks.

He wheels at anchor now, in his element,
and sometimes he floats free of the dry world
in that narrow white boat
that is going nowhere, wreathed in steam.
And sometimes he remembers her.

'Washing you,' he murmurs, as the green water
laps his body. 'Remember washing you.'
His eyes are screwed shut.
His arms are folded across his chest
as if he is flying into himself.

DOCK LEAVES

(1994)

Post-War British

Everyone screwing up their eyes
as if they can't quite make us out –
Jim with his hair fully restored,
Johnny with the Simoniz duster,
polishing the Jowett Javelin to extinction
as long ago as 1951.

There's no such person as Anne,
but Gar is still there, looking quite like
her old self again, and Mr Burns,
none the worse for New Zealand,
waiting for us to make up our minds:
are we coming with them or not?

The afternoon goes on like that
until we are piling into the car,
trying not to sit in the middle.
Isn't that the anti-carsick chain
hanging down behind, that was supposed to
earth the static electricity?

It doesn't even touch the ground!
The children leaning out of the windows
must be waving goodbye
to their own grandchildren,
but they think they can smell the sea
just over the next horizon.

And here we all are at last –
our faces coming up tired but satisfied
at the other end of our lives,
our knitted bathing-trunks falling down.

The cross-hatched anti-invasion groynes
postmark the scene for us in 1948

and all the dogs that existed then,
named after Sid Field characters,
leaping to within an inch of the stick
that hovers in the air above the sea,
bring it back to us now
and lay it at our feet.

On Our Marks

I start furthest back
on the yew tree path, crouching down,
my fingers touching the earth.
My brother comes next,
just far enough ahead to give me a race.
Our sister, nearest home,
looks over her shoulder at us,
knowing she will probably win.

At the end of the path you stand,
one hand holding up a yellow handkerchief.
We wait on our marks,
our hearts beating faster now, our eyes
fixed on your upraised hand,
the handkerchief fluttering in the wind.

A Dam

My mother calls my name,
a familiar, two-note sound
that carries across the fields
and finds me here,
kneeling beside a stream,
my arms plunged up to the elbows in mud.

I make my way back to the house
and try to explain
what I've been doing all this time
so far away from home.
'Making dams?' she will ask.
'Or making poems about making dams?'

Standstill

A last visit to the long-abandoned 'Gosses' on Harold Macmillan's
Birch Grove estate, soon to be levelled as part of a new golf course.

I apologize to the driver
for the branches closing in,
almost bringing us to a standstill.
He doesn't seem to mind.
'I'm like you,' he tells me, as we move aside
a tree blown across the drive by the storm.
'I had to come back home
to see my own particular corner of the UK
before I died. Our daughter wanted to stay out there
in New Zealand and get married.
Don't ask me why.
She's a karate champion.'

We have turned a corner in the drive, past the swing,
past the gibbet, past the tree
where we buried the screaming idol's head
of Elsie Byers, the American agent.
Flowering creepers and bushes
crowd round the old house,
as if some great party were being given there
long ago, the party of the season.
Look, the same door! The same knocker!
The same doorhandle I held
when I came back from going round the world!
The same footscraper!

The driver seems to share my astonishment
that everything is the same yet different
when you look through a window
into your old room
and see your head lying on the pillow,
innocent of your life, but dreaming your dreams.
'Where is it you say old Supermac used to live?
I want to see the field
where President Kennedy landed in his helicopter.
I was cheering and waving the American flag.
Our daughter had just been born. We were on our way
to start a new life in New Zealand.'

Margaret Vyner

1925. Paris passes from high Anglophilia to unbridled
Negromania. The Charleston is born. Women bob
their hair, smoke cigarettes, embark on love affairs.
The couturier Jean Patou creates three new scents to

evoke the three great moments of love: 'Amour Amour', 'Que Sais-Je?', 'Adieu Sagesse'. On the other side of the world, in Winona, Sydney, a skinny eleven-year-old girl called Margaret Vyner walks through a plate glass window and amazes everyone by escaping unhurt.

1927. Lindberg crosses the Atlantic. The Surrealist Gallery opens in Paris. From a boutique on the beach at Deauville, Jean Patou launches 'le sportswear'. He dresses tennis star Suzanne Lenglen. The suntanned look is *à la mode* and Patou is the first to introduce suntan oil to the world. It is called 'Chaldée'. In Australia, outdoor girl Margaret Vyner enters Ascham School for Girls, where the uniform is a disappointing beige, like everyone's permanently tanned skin.

1929. Diaghilev dies. Black Friday on Wall Street. For Paris society it is the high summer of ostentation and elegant extravagance. The last wave of desperate optimism inspires Patou's homage in perfume to a generation: 'Moment Suprême'. A gawky fifteen, Margaret Vyner is attending the dancing classes of Alexei Dolinoff, who came to Australia with Pavlova and also teaches Robert Helpmann. Her only despair is that she has grown too tall to be a ballet dancer.

1930. Gandhi comes to Europe. Picasso is awarded the Carnegie Prize. René Clair shoots the first talkie on the roofs of Paris. In the salons of Patou's *hotel particulier* in the Rue St Florentin, a cocktail bar has been opened for the benefit of customers. In recognition of the new decade's sophistication, he has mixed his 'Cocktail' range of scents, bright and fresh as an aperitif. In

Sydney, the budding sixteen-year-old is starting to be toasted.

1933. The Bauhaus closes its doors. Pierre Bonnard paints *Le Grand Nu au Miroir*. In America, conserves of pickled rattlesnake go on sale. In Paris, Patou's 'Divine Folie' captures the mood of the moment as one mad craze follows another into oblivion. Margaret Vyner is touring Australia and New Zealand as a chorus girl in the musical comedy *Flora Dora*. Her divine folly is a plan to run away to Europe.

1934. Miss Vyner arrives in Paris with no money, no French and no contacts. She attends a Jean Patou dress show for fun and is instantly offered a modelling job by the vigilant couturier. He takes her to dinner in the Bois de Boulogne and then on to the lesbian night-club Le Monocle, where the virginal Australian orders her usual glass of milk.

1935. The liner SS *Normandie* breaks the record for the Atlantic crossing: four days, two hours, twelve minutes. Later the same year, Patou launches his own version of 'Normandie': a spell blended of sea and the voyage, bound with that special sense of bewildered luxury. Margaret Vyner is photographed in nautical mood at the party to launch the fragrance on board the SS *Normandie* at Cherbourg.

1936. June 19: total eclipse of the sun. Sacha Guitry introduces 'Le Mot de Cambronne' to polite society (General Cambronne is reputed to have uttered '*Merde*' when asked to surrender at Waterloo), while the French government introduces paid holidays to the people. 'Why does the air smell so sweet when I wake in the morning?' Paul Poiret asks Patou. 'What is that subtle flavour of dawn, as if the whole garden has poured into my room?' 'It is the fragrance that has just been created by Patou,' replies Patou. 'And it is called "Vacances".' Margaret Vyner tours his Collection to Lyons, Dijon, Deauville, Biarritz and Cannes. Then flies to Croydon Airport for the next stage of her adventure.

1938. Matisse paints *Le Jardin d'Hiver*. Le Corbusier draws up his plans for the urbanization of Buenos Aires. The skies look threatening over Europe. Rumours of war are mixed with dreams of escape. In this loaded atmosphere, Patou-Prospero summons up his 'Colony' – a scent evocative of sun-ripened fruit and beautiful Creole women in blue-plumed head-dresses. In London, our colonial friend has wangled herself the part of someone's girlfriend in a Broadway-bound Freddy Lonsdale play, *Once is Enough*, in order to meet its leading man, Hugh Williams. The first evening on board the SS *Washington*, he sends a note to her table, 'Champagne better than milk. Why don't you join me?' She is soon weaned.

1939. Auden and Isherwood leave England for America. Hugh Williams and Margaret Vyner pawn his mother's mink for a last pre-war holiday on Capri. On September 3 she is sitting in a basket rehearsing Terence Rattigan's *French Without Tears* when she hears the news that war has been declared. The party is over.

1946. Sinatra fever. René Simon opens his acting school in Paris. Death of Gertrude Stein and actor

Raimu. Jean Patou's new scent, 'L'Heure Attendue',
celebrates the longed-for Liberation with an access of
joy for the rebirth of his beloved Paris. On the Left
Bank, a new world is stammering into existence. It is
the epic poem known as St-Germain-des-Près. On the
other side of the Channel, I never go anywhere
without my mother's empty Patou scent bottle in the
shape of a crown.

The Fall

My father lived in the Garden of Allah,
an exotic, bungalow-style hotel
which Thomas Wolfe told Scott Fitzgerald
he could not believe existed, even in Hollywood.
He was sacked by Paramount after serving only
one year of a five-year contract
when his first three films made the Critics'
Ten Worst Films list for 1934.
He heard the news of his redundancy
when the Studio called him at the Garden
and told him they had 2,400 signed publicity stills
he might like to take home with him.

I found them thirty years later,
stuck together from damp in an old vanity case.
Almost everything about him had changed,
if it ever really existed.
The toothbrush moustache, slightly curled,
recalled the Garden of Allah, long since demolished
by the Lytton Loan and Savings Company
to make way for another tower block.

The Company left behind a model of the Garden
to mark the spot where it had stood on Sunset Blvd.
I went looking for the model in 1975,
but it too had disappeared without trace.

The Phoney War

The Army contrived to enter
a wide range of deductions
for this particular week.
No one got much above ten shillings.
Your father, I remember,
whose debts to the Inland Revenue
amounted to four figures,
received, incredulously, about 8/6.
He had placed the coins on the railway line
and let a train pass over them,
so that they were larger, thinner,
and completely valueless.

According to the Sergeant Major
he would have been burnt to a cinder
when he set his foot
on the live rail we'd heard so much about,
if it hadn't been for the toe-caps
on his boots, or the fact that
his bayonet wasn't fixed.
Everyone except your father
had some theory or other
why he was lucky to be still alive
guarding Staines Railway Bridge
during the Phoney War.

War and Peace

'The hotel has been opened up as an officers' rest place
and the *boule* table dug up from the cellar.
Nobody to run the thing, so Hugh Fraser and I
borrowed all the ready we could lay our hands on
and started crouping like crazy. Everything was fine
until we got smacked for 800 francs in a single coup.
Ugly moments followed as IOUs were hastily written
and Robin Baring despatched to the camp
to fetch the profits from the men's canteen.
I was terrified and Hugh looked very white and sweaty,
as we had no idea how we could fix the canteen money.
Robin returned and we redeemed our IOUs, then,
by the grace of God, the Navy arrived, determined
to wipe us out. We recouped completely, something like
eleven mille and made about 800 each. Next morning
there was a notice in the Mess: "Until further notice
Officers will not run the bank at Boule."
So we've arranged for the Grenadiers to take it over.'

The war used up the last of my father's winning streak
and sent him home to face the music.
The Inland Revenue were waiting behind the door.
'If you do this to me now,' he told the Tax Inspector,
'I'll leave this bloody country and never come back.'
The following week they took away his passport.
After six years in the Army, looking forward to all this,
he's standing guard by his bedroom window,
keeping watch for the landlord's Jaguar.
He rubs an invisible coin between finger and thumb,
twists his signet ring round and round with circular
reasoning. He would like to slip through the ring

and disappear, but his family is watching and waiting
to see what he will do next. He jumps to his feet
and goes on frantic, all-night house hunting missions
on the Green Line bus. He came home one morning
in a taxi, holding up two cards, a jack and a nine,
his winning hand in a game of *chemin de fer*.

Elephants

'A mix of feelings came to me
when I saw your father's photograph in the *Guardian*
and read the text of your article.
Warm recollections of Tam as I knew him
in a camp on a hillside in Tunisia,
gratitude at my good fortune in having known him,
then sadness at being told you were only just beginning
to talk to one another when he died.

'It was a strong enough mixture to make me write to you.
I shall certainly get your book,
but I wanted to say that as a young officer in Phantom
I met an array of self-confident (outwardly),
able and/or aristocratic young men,
who came from a different world from my own.
I learnt a lot from conversations on politics and philosophy
between Christopher Mayhew and Hugh Fraser,

'I watched your father playing backgammon
for what I thought incredible stakes
and my Scottish Presbyterian background was fascinated
and repelled by language and attitudes
that were not mine. Tam's sensitivity to my thoughts,

his courtesy and warmth and unmalicious humour,
made him a sort of serene, poised hero for me,
so different was your apprehension of him.

'Just after the surrender of the German army in Tunisia
he and I and another were in Carthage
"emptying the ashtrays and counting the broken
glasses".
Tam did a one-man act of getting elephants
on board ship for Hannibal's expedition to Italy.
One of us pointed out that Hannibal had gone by way
of Tangiers.
Immediately Tam shouted out, "Cancel, change of
orders",
and went through a one-man unloading act quite
brilliantly.'

Last Goodbyes

On the last day of the holidays
we are dying men,
remembering our lost youth
in the rhododendron trees.
We say goodbye to the henhouse,
the potting shed, the flat roof,
the island with a drawbridge.
We have our last go on the swing
with the table underneath
for launching ourselves off into space.
We swing in a great circle,
pushing ourselves away from the tree
with our feet, till we spin

giddily back to the table again –
all afternoon, till it is time to go.
On the last day of the holidays
we stand completely still,
waiting for the taxi to come,
remembering our lost youth
in the rhododendron trees.

The Age of Steam

Remember porters? Weatherbeaten old boys
with watery blue eyes
who were never around when you wanted them?
You had to find one
before you could go anywhere in 1953.
It was part of saying goodbye.
Quick, darling, run and find a porter
while I get your ticket.
I'll meet you at the barrier.

I run off across the station forecourt
in a series of sudden dashes,
panicky knight moves
which leave my head spinning
as I glance over my shoulder at my trunk.
Inside are my darts, my throwing-knife set,
my signalling torch, my *True Romance* magazines –
everything I need to survive
in the months ahead, even my compass.

There are no porters anywhere,
only JADS, assistant head,

standing over by the barrier,
jingling the change in his pocket.
Report to the Master-on-Duty.
Collect your sheets.
Put away your things on the right shelf.

My mother appears like a new sun
from behind a cloud. She is smiling now,
as if to welcome me home.
She has a porter in tow.
I won't wait, darling.
You know how I hate goodbyes.
You've got your comics and your cars.
I've written to you . . .

A last gasp of *Moment Suprême*
as she leans over me, then nothing at all
but the ribbon of her smell unravelling,
the station clock moving on with a little jerk,
the whistle blowing.

This is it, then – the great leap backwards
into make-believe, the covered wagons
drawn in a circle on the dusty plain,
flaming tomahawks flying through the air.

Joy

Not so much a sting
as a faint burn

not so much a pain
as the memory of pain

the memory of tears
flowing freely down cheeks

in a sort of joy
that there was nothing

worse in all the world
than stinging nettle stings

and nothing better
than cool dock leaves.

Lights Out

We're allowed to talk for ten minutes
about what has happened during the day,
then we have to go to sleep.
It doesn't matter what we dream about.

A Blockage

Can you write a letter
saying I don't have to have brawn?
You can see the bristles in it
and pieces of bone.

And can you write a letter
saying when you are coming down?
If you write on Monday
I'll get it on Tuesday

and can use the envelope
to smuggle it out of the dining room.
After supper on Tuesdays
there is a big queue for the lavatories.

Last week there was a blockage
and all the brawn was found
stuck together. When you come down
can we go and see the model village?

Old Boy

Our lesson is really idiotic today,
as if Mr Ray has forgotten
everything he ever knew
about the Reformation
and is making it up as he goes along.

I feel like pointing out
where he's going astray,
but I'm frightened he'll hold up
some of my grey hair
and accuse me of cheating.

How embarrassing
if I turned out to be wrong after all
and Mr Ray was right. Luckily,
I'm in the top class
and come top easily, without trying,
the way it should be.

I could do better
in the written answer questions,

but everyone looks up to me
because I've been round the world
and have my own wife and motorbike.

I'm wearing my old school scarf
that I thought was lost forever.
Brown and magenta quarters,
the smartest colours in the world.
It was round my neck all the time.

Visitants

I went back the other day
to collect my motorbike
from the local police station.
I couldn't believe
that lonely northern outpost
where I went to school
was barely half an hour
from London by train:

not far away and long ago
as I had imagined,
but facing the future
surrounded by Kodak bungalows
and flyovers,
its dreaded Tower
a little spiral staircase
with geraniums in window boxes.

I skidded on the gravel
outside the headmaster's study,
shot round the side

past the library, the Chapel,
the 'Private Side',
hoping to escape without being seen
via the tradesmen's entrance
into Locker's Lane.

Blocking my path,
clipboard and pen at the ready,
stood JADS, brick-faced
Classics master and assistant head,
shouting my name
and bearing down on me,
exactly the same
as when he was alive.

The Accident

The cricket ball lingered an eternity
in the patch of blue sky
before returning eventually to earth.

I was standing with outstretched arms
when the full force of the future
hit me in the mouth.

Man and Superman

A dedicated student of the play –
that was my father's vision
of his start in life. 'When I was your age
I'd seen everything in London.
I read plays for fun.
I queued half way down the Strand
to see Barrymore and du Maurier
in *Man and Superman*.
I sat in the gallery
with the book open on my knee ...'

It didn't happen that way.
His widowed mother
was a Gallery First Nighter
who took him along with her
to all the popular
star vehicles of the day
and told him he was handsome.
He failed the Army Exam
and went to RADA for a year
to meet women.

When I spun my line
about wanting to do the same
he hit the roof. 'I suppose you think
you'd be famous overnight
and make pots of money. Well, you might.
But then again you might not.
It's my job to think of things like that.
Tell me honestly,
how many plays in London
have you actually seen?'

I clenched my fists under the table
and muttered something about television.
I didn't want to work.
I didn't want to act.
I wanted to make him laugh.
I told him the one about the constipated airman
and said the last thing first
and had to start again.
His lip came out. His jaw went slack.
'It's rather unfunny, isn't it?'

I'm Your Father, Remember?

I used to think he was naturally like that –
imperious, categorical, always in the wrong
and rightly so, the only man in the world
who could talk about opera and French mustard
as if they were the same sort of thing,
banging the table, saying 'Come off it, old boy!
I'm your father, remember?' – clapping his hands
and when a waiter busied round his chair, saying
'Steady on, you're not a knife-thrower.
Now go out to the kitchen and start again.'
When I stole a comb from the Gentlemen's in the Savoy
he made me take it back. If I'd only murdered
the attendant, all would have been forgiven.
I used to think he was naturally like that.

Four Plays by Hugh and Margaret Williams

1

My mother's mink came out of long-term hock
for the first night
of *Plaintiff in a Pretty Hat.*
Its sprinkling of grey hairs
caught the light
in the foyer of the St Martin's
on the cover of *Theatregoer* magazine
for Christmas 1955. Its glow
of new-found confidence signalled an end
to bankruptcy and woe.

2

It would turn up next
as a character
in their only Broadway success,
The Grass is Greener.
An American millionaire
walks through the wrong door
of a stately home
and falls in love with the Countess.
He wants to give her a mink, a wild one,
without her husband (my father)
finding out about their affair.
They hit on the idea
of a cloakroom ticket
found in a taxi,
but the husband turns the tables on them.
The suitcase flies open
and out falls a cricket bat,

three old cricket pads
and a string of flags.
The couple take hold of the string
and start pulling out the flags as
THE CURTAIN FALLS.

3

The mink would earn its grey hairs
at various first nights and premières
throughout the Sixties,
till my parents came up with their
anti-fur-trade comedy,
The Irregular Verb To Love.
Hedda, my father's theatrical wife,
gets herself arrested
for putting a fire-bomb through the letter-box
of a furriers. The mink was obviously
guilty of something, but what?

4

Demoted from love object
to scapegoat, from one
production to the next,
it could hardly attend the première
of its own burning
and went into hiding
as the lining of my father's
'ultimate winter coat' –
the one he wore
for his own last winter, endlessly touring,
waiting to come into London
with *His, Hers and Theirs*, their last

[216]

light comedy about divorce.
He would leave it behind
in his dressing-room that Spring,
a headless ghost, an exit line,
a pelt on a stick. My mother's mink
has gone back to storage in my father's head.

Early Morning Swim

Every year now you make your face
a little fainter in its vellum photo-frame,
as if you were washing off your make-up with a towel
and catching the last train home.

You have forgotten how to storm
and shout about the place, but not how to gaze
abstractedly over our shoulders into this room
that is not your room any more.

What do you see that we don't see? Why don't you mind
if we are late coming down to breakfast,
or we don't ring up as much as we should?
At this distance, your voice grows fainter on the line,

your words harder to catch. With one hand
you shield your eyes from the sun, as if you have decided
to overlook the way we dress to come up to London
or go to the theatre. You can't see me,

but I can see you, walking away from us, throwing back
your shoulders as you breathe the sea air,
pretending not to limp over the rocky ground.
It is early morning, time for our early morning swim.

You lead the way in your towelling dressing-gown
down the alley behind the hotel, us two boys
sleep-walking along behind you, stumbling
and grumbling a little because it is so early.

We don't understand that this could be our last
swim together, our last chance to prove that we are men.
We don't want to go of course, but we do really.
The water will be cold at this time of day.

Truce

I woke in my clothes
and made my way downstairs.
The house was quiet,
like the memory of a house.
The furniture was thin, provisional,
ranged against the wall.

My father was standing under a lightbulb,
eating a sausage
dipped in horseradish sauce.
I helped myself to Shredded Wheat and a banana.
We stood on the verandah together
and peed on the daffodils.

Dinner with My Mother

My mother is saying 'Now'.
'Now,' she says, taking down a saucepan,
putting it on the stove.
She doesn't say anything else for a while,

so that time passes slowly, on the simmer,
until it is 'Now' again
as she hammers out our steaks
for Steak Diane.

I have to be on hand at times like this
for table-laying,
drink replenishment
and general conversational encouragement,

but I am getting hungry
and there is nowhere to sit down.
'Now,' I say, making a point
of opening a bottle of wine.

My mother isn't listening.
She's miles away,
testing the sauce with a spoon,
narrowing her eyes through the steam.

'Now,' she says very slowly, meaning
which is it to be,
the rosemary or the tarragon vinegar
for the salad dressing?

I hold my breath, lest anything
should go wrong at the last minute.

But now it is really 'Now',
our time to sit and eat.

Algarve, 1991

World Service

Ten to four and the World Service still on upstairs,
which means that you are sleeping well again tonight,
which means that it got you off to sleep
and hasn't yet woken you again.
The sound of waves from the sea at the foot of the cliff
washes over the voices coming and going in waves.
A motor scooter starts up, then fizzles out again.

I can't sleep, so I get up and look out of the window
onto the dim-lit esplanade, where one or two couples
are finding their way home from the clubs.
I feel jealous and sad, but I like to see them,
lingering at discreet intervals under the palm trees.
Out at sea, the last fishing boats are coming in,
their big lamps slung below the horizon like stars.

For a moment, the broadcast voice upstairs
rises above the waves, insistent, incoherent, cracked.
You wake yourself and manage to reach out a hand
to switch it off. 6.30 and the World Service is quiet,
which means that you are sleeping well again tonight.
Far below, the beach tractor ploughs back and forth,
readying the beach for another day.

Algarve, 1992

Holiday Poem

Some little bird near here
is going 'What? What? What?' all the time,
as if he can't understand what I am saying.
O what is the matter little bird?
Why can't you relax for a moment in the sun
the way I am doing, sing a song,
enjoy the day for what it is?
'What? What? What? What? What?'

The sun is out, clouds are flying past on boards,
chickens are pecking at windfalls,
grasshoppers hum. The pears aren't ripe,
but the apple branches are so full of apples
they are being held up by wooden poles.
Why don't you try one?
What harm could it possibly do?
'What? What? What? What? What? What?'

Bird, I am here and you are there
and everything, for the time being at least,
is all right with the world.
You have got the run of your teeth
and I have got a cup of tea, a good book
and someone I love to sit with.
What more could anyone ask?
'What? What? What? What? What? What? What?'

Safe

Remember the days when six things happened every
   night
and no one wore an overcoat to go out?
Turning your back on a planned evening with friends
you felt the world opening its arms. The triple miracle
of meeting, liking, being liked, was taken for granted
on the way back to her flat.

I feel ashamed tonight, checking the fires are out,
checking the alarm is on, checking the bed is tucked in,
that I am not really old, or ill, or tired,
only sensible. Whatever it is
that goes click-clacking past the end of the street
makes me draw the curtains and call it a rainy night.

A Look

of 'How could you do this to me?'
was written all over her face,

which he knew very well would soon
be written all over his own.

A Lap of Honour

The front door bangs
and I creep downstairs in my dressing-gown,
unable to believe my good luck.
It is like Christmas morning long ago,

the fields all white,
the day like an unopened present.

I can do whatever I like.
I can move the furniture back against the wall.
I can dance a jig in the hall.
I can sit completely still
reading a book about Aristotle.
I can do nothing at all.

Later on, I sit down to supper with myself,
having opened a bottle of wine.
I touch my glass to the TV screen
in a toast to the BBC.
My house is your house, old friend!
Stay switched on all the time if you want to.

With a glass in my hand
I make the tour of my property –
a lap of honour to celebrate my victory.
As I cruise the house, humming to myself,
I set things in motion as I pass,
curtains and cups and kitchen implements

sway to and fro at my touch,
even the chandelier swings back and forth
in cheerful valediction to absent friends.
A birdcage hanging from the ceiling
tolls like a bell
for my new found liberation.

Saturday Morning

Everyone who made love the night before
was walking around with flashing red lights
on top of their heads – a white-haired old gentleman,
a red-faced schoolboy, a pregnant woman
who smiled at me from across the street
and gave a little secret shrug,
as if the flashing red light on her head
was a small price to pay for what she knew.

Prayer

God give me strength to lead a double life.
Cut me in half.
Make each half happy in its own way
with what is left. Let me disobey
my own best instincts
and do what I want to do, whatever that may be,
without regretting it, or thinking I might.

When I come home late at night from home,
saying I have to go away,
remind me to look out the window
to see which house I'm in.
Pin a smile on my face
when I turn up two weeks later with a tan
and presents for everyone.

Teach me how to stand and where to look
when I say the words
about where I've been

and what sort of time I've had.
Was it good or bad or somewhere in between?
I'd like to know how I feel about these things,
perhaps you'd let me know?

When it's time to go to bed in one of my lives,
go ahead of me up the stairs,
shine a light in the corners of my room.
Tell me this: do I wear pyjamas here,
or sleep with nothing on?
If you can't oblige by cutting me in half,
God give me strength to lead a double life.

Static

Meeting again after so long
we scanned our hearts
for the tell-tale static to register.

The impatient scribble of midges
on the evening air?
Or the fine pencil lines of rain?

Faith

After we broke up
and agreed not to call or write
for at least a year,
I found myself drawn
for a little comfort and cheer
not so much to the top shelf

of W. H. Smith
with its flesh-tinted offers
of doom and gloom,

as the bra and knicker counter
of Marks & Spencer,
where row upon row
of carefully labelled
dream-tatters
in chocolate and dusky peach
seemed to encourage
a humorous approach
and faith in a providing world.

Poetry

Ten, no, five seconds
after coming all
over the place
too soon,

I was lying there
wondering
where to put the
line-breaks in.

Message Not Left on an Answerphone

for C.

As night comes on, I remember we used to play
at this time of day, and you would tell me:
'Don't get excited now, or we'll miss the film.'
You would be sitting on my lap, making a fuss of me.
A shoulder strap would fall down.
A buckle would come away in my hand.
That famous buckle! Did you get it mended yet?
Sometimes the telephone would ring
while we were playing, making us cross,
even though it was still quite early.
You would pick up the phone and talk noncommittally
for a moment or two, because you had to.
How I loved you when you talked like that.
At other times we let the answerphone do the work
and listened to the names of your friends
coming through from another world.
Darling, we made ourselves late sometimes,
playing those games. We made ourselves cry.
Now it is me who hangs endlessly on the line,
who hears your voice repeating at all hours:
'I can't get to the phone at the moment,
but do leave a message.' Pick up the phone, damn you.
Can't you recognize one of my silences by now?

In the Blindfold Hours

In the blindfold hours,
in the memory wars,
don't fool yourself it never happened,
that you never loved her.
Don't degrade yourself with empty hopes like these.

Go to the window. Listen to the trees.
It is only air we live in.
There is nothing to be frightened of.

Keats

How can I find love in the middle of the night
when the only females out so late
are rag mountains scavenging the bins
behind Indian restaurants? Imagine a dog kennel
made out of old audio cartons. Inside sits a thing
lagged in pink polystyrene, tickling her palm,
blowing out her cheeks at me. She shows me
her business card, an empty sardine tin
attached to a chain round her neck.

I spring forth eagerly, excited by the smell
of sardine oil clinging to her fur. I want to do it
immediately on the pile of old yoghurt pots
and take-away boxes, but she makes me wait
while she slips into something different to go out –
a sheath made of 'I'm Backing Britain' shopping bags,
a veil made of tarred and knotted string.

Like a gigantic hen, she leads the way down Oxford St,
tapping on plate glass windows with a twig.

Madame Charmaine

I see the board with a pencil
for contributions to the flowers
has gone up outside No. 8.
It must be the hairdresser,
the sculptress in lacquer, the part-time
spiritualist who devised her own
special effects – bloodstains and bumps
and lights going on and off
in the upstairs salon
that doubled as a seance chamber.

I used to visit Madame Charmaine
in the long-haired era before last
to have my hair left alone,
my ear bitten by her macaw.
When she died, a life-sized
papier-mâché model was found
sitting with her in the salon.
Hanks of human hair had been stuck to
its scalp and backcombed
into a sugary helmet like her own.

Soft Porn

Her towel is an island she is cast up on
in attitudes of sleep or abandon,
or screwing up her eyes against the light,
as if she has woken in the middle of the night
and come downstairs to find us all still up
and glanced around her with her mouth quite slack
and fiddled with a string behind her back.

See how she lowers her body to the sand,
kneeling, with one leg stretched behind,
twisting and turning until she gets it right,
presenting different aspects to our sight,
her sex obscured, in case we had forgotten,
by a picture of itself in cotton,
and now and then a pair of tits all white.

We feel ourselves going down without a fight,
plummeting earthwards from a great height,
but we triumph over it with a loud shout,
walking around with our tummies sticking out,
turning our heads from left to right,
admiring the way the waves go in and out,
and now and then a pair of tits all white.

Holiday's End

We leave the villa early, carrying toys,
and drift down to the beach for hangovers.
(There was sand in the bed, one of us didn't sleep.)
Every time we look up, scanning the horizon for a sign,

another package screams behind the mountain,
another sailboard hits the ocean.

A vast departure lounge surrounds us with Duty Free,
Pink Floyd on the seafront p.a., time-share cowboys.
As we lie back, closing our eyes, we are fastening
our seat-belts, putting out our cigarettes, touching down.
The front door we are trying to push open
is snagged with next year's brochures.

*

The treasured routine now briefly no longer treasured,
the long-distance holiday-makers drag their feet
through the stubble fields overhanging the sea.
In the fading light they have left behind a face-mask,
whose curved breathing tubes stick up out of the sand
like the horns of a lost war-helm.

Ireland Swings

1

Flushed with the success
of 'Young Love'
and his placing in *New Spotlight*'s
Top Ten Band Poll,
Donnie Collins sipped a cool lager
in the reception area
of the Hotel Arcadia, Bray,
and told me frankly:
'More than the Poll,
the most important aspect

of the new disc
is the number of radio plays
it receives – that's the only
real test of a record
and the only true yardstick
by which anyone can measure
the impact of a number.'

Brian Coll, whose cover version
of 'England Swings'
is currently sneaking up
the Irish charts, agreed with him
that radio exposure
can make or break a record.
His 'Ireland Swings'
has all the ingredients
of a monster hit for Brian,
plus a steady demand for it
in the shops. He told me:
'The air of the tune
is sufficiently well known
and the fact that a lot of
towns are mentioned on the disc
gives it a colloquial flavour
which should pay off handsomely.'

2

As everyone knows by now,
Dickie and Rowland Soper
are travelling together
to Luxembourg,
where Dickie will be singing
Ireland's entry

in the Eurovision Song Contest,
with brother Rowland producing.
No one is predicting
just how successful
the lads will be,
but whatever the outcome,
one thing is certain,
back home in Ireland
'Come Back to Stay'
is sure to be one of the year's
biggest sellers
and a moneyspinner
for Rowland and Dickie.
So good luck to them!

3

It isn't easy stepping into your father's shoes
when the shoes in question belong to Jack Ruane.
Yet that is precisely what Jack Junior has done
and Pops is delighted. Of course, Jack Senior
was a household name on the international circuit
long before most of his fans were even born.
From New York to New Ross, from the days of the
foxtrot to the rhythm-and-blues era, he built up
a steady following among the dance-hall crowd,
who never missed one of his Latin American dates
at the Hotel Arcadia. Recently, however, he has been
obliged to give up the band for health reasons
and hand over the reins of leadership to his son,
who has promised to carry on the great tradition.

4

Like most other showbands
The Hoedowners have had their
share of teething troubles
over the years.
The eponymous TV series
which should have
relaunched their career
proved a mixed blessing.
Old wags shook their heads
and predicted the group
would be just another
bunch of also-rans
on the scrapheap of history.

All that has changed.
With their new disc release,
'Showball Crazy',
a bright new star has emerged
and taken his place
alongside the image idols.
His name is Sean Dunphy
and he is a natural.
Now even the knockers have to admit
the ex-carpenter from Co. Clare
has chipped his way
into the ranks
of musical greatness.

5

I've seen them all
in the square jungle

that is the boxing ring
of Dublin's National Stadium,
boxers and singers,
rockers and rollers,
supergroups and no-hopers,
from Gus Farrell to Seamus Dunphy,
from Dickie Rock to Spider Murphy,
but none of them
could hold a candle
to the scintillating Dixies,
the knock-out showband
with the punchy beat.

It was the occasion
of *New Spotlight*'s
promotion of the show
to aid the Central Remedial Clinic
and it was a sell-out.
Ballads and blues we had in full
and I liked them all.
Mary Flynn and Mary Byrne,
the Wolfe Tones were there
with Father Joseph on drums.
The Creatures impressed
with their spirited antics.
The Action had their
followers out in force.

Murty Quinn and Chris Grace
highlighted the first half
with their great rendition
of 'Nothing to Lose'.
The Stadium was bopping
to the swinging sound,

[235]

but the fabulous Dixies
were the daddies of them all.
Across the ring they strutted
like court jesters:
zany Joe, sturdy Chris,
hefty Steve and clean-cut Brendan.
It was the wildest reception
I have ever seen at the venue.

Waiting to Go On

When I hear the five-minute call
for Orchestra and Beginners
I take my chair upstairs
and sit in the wings in my underpants,
my trousers over one arm.
I'm not in the first scene,
but I don't trust the Tannoy any more
after what happened the other night.
'If you're not coming on, Mr Williams,
that's all right with me,
but for God's sake don't come on late.'

They let the first Walking Gentleman go
after only one warning
just for lying down between the Acts.
They didn't bother auditioning the part,
they recast the suit
and I happened to have short arms.
It's cold sitting here night after night
with nothing over my knees,
but the suit belongs to the Company

and I don't want to be fined
for having poor creases.

Mirth

The lights come up, the stage is bare,
the audience goes on sitting there,

row upon row of gleaming teeth,
set in expressions of dutiful mirth

for something they have long since forgotten.
Someone has spilled an ice-cream cone

from the Balcony onto someone's head.
It trickles down over his forehead

and from there down into his lap.
We see the smile fade from his lips,

the lips fade from his mouth,
The mouth slowly wither from his teeth.

Now his jaw drops open on its tendons
and a look of horrified understanding dawns.

The urge to clap is irresistible.
He finds this is no longer possible.

Leakage

Muscle patterns that show satisfaction or delight
as opposed to a disingenuous smirk

have been identified by the Laboratory of Human
    Interaction
to provide more information about suicidal patients
who want to check themselves out of hospital
in order to take their own lives.

The best test for a genuine smile
is to look at the eyebrow and watch for skin droop.
The skin under the eyebrow is lowered only in genuine
    smiles.
Unhappy feelings show through false smiles
for about one third of a second
in what we term 'leakage'.

Everyone Knows This

Every object, every action,
a light suddenly switched on,
a door left open,
carries a hidden watermark
of joy or joylessness,
hope or hopelessness,
which might reveal itself
in the look on someone's face.

Children crying in the next door house,
young men going to work,
the saxophone solo
in 'I'm Gonna Be a Wheel Some Day',
are sorrowful or reassuring
depending on a smell of garlic

drifting up from downstairs,
or the sound of a horse race.

We live in a tiny place
where everything is attached
to something else, more precious.
Dog-barks, head-shakes,
unexpected knocks
bring tears to our eyes.
A box of Brillo pads
comes close to happiness.

The Sea

i.m. K.S.

When I am with you, I am a minute behind,
picking up pieces of coloured glass
and calling you back to me, 'Look ...'

You have seen something new up ahead.
You don't look round. There you go,
scrambling over rocks on your way to the sea.

In My Absence

Provide a short piece of writing about your life.
It doesn't have to be a long, rambling account,
saying what you think it all means,
just something you could read out to our members,
or which could be read out in your absence.

Untitled

O tender two-note songs without refrains,
don't I remember you?
Haven't I waited till now
for you to come round once more,
holding out to me like hands
those frail, forgiving themes?

It makes me tremble to know
I wasted so many days.
My thirst for you
lies buried in the lake,
which reaches out to me hands I can't touch,
a life I can't drink from or break.

After the Writing Course

A few white plastic chairs
placed here and there
in writerly seclusion,
or huddling in pairs,
recall a life of excited
rivalry lived here
as recently as yesterday.
The lime tree has let fall
hundreds of little
floating contraptions,
which parade around the swimming pool
in great irregular crowds.
Out of habit, I note
how each individual

raft-like structure
has a mast and mainsail
which propel it confidently
towards an uncertain future.

Last Poem

I have put on a grotesque mask
to write these lines. I sit
staring at myself
in a mirror propped on my desk.

I hold up my head
like one of those Chinese lanterns
hollowed out of a pumpkin,
swinging from a broom.

I peer through the eye-holes
into that little lighted room
where a candle burns,
making me feel drowsy.

I must try not to spill the flame
wobbling in its pool of wax.
It sheds no light on the scene,
only shadows flickering up the walls.

In the narrow slit of my mouth
my tongue appears,
darting back and forth
behind the bars of my teeth.

I incline my head,
to try and catch what I am saying.
No sound emerges, only
the coming and going of my breath.

BILLY'S RAIN

(1999)

Silver Paper Men

They exist in rudimentary gardens,
flourishing a cane or twirling a parasol,
all nipped-in waists, doffed hats
and little pointed shoes.
Regency bucks and belles,
they appear out of nowhere, for no reason,
leaning by a bridge or balustrade,
admiring a willow tree.
Given over to reflection,
they do nothing for a season, in pairs,
while a butterfly waits in mid-air.
That impossible basket of flowers
says all there is to say about love
in their shiny black world.

After dark, their silver paper costumes
shimmer in the light from the street.
Their flickering afterimages
stiff-leg-it round the room
in time to some tinselly tune from long ago.
For a moment, they seem to dance together.
Suddenly bashful, they hide
behind fans or dance programmes,
or turn their heads to one side.
They pass their days like this,
bowing and scraping to one another
on either side of a mantelpiece or door,
till one of them goes missing,
or crashes to the floor.

Anything

It might have been the word for sulking in animals,
Juliette Lewis, Joan of Arc, the smell
of television lingering in the morning like a quarrel.
It might have been an Airedale scratching at your door,
papier-mâché heads, a cloud no bigger than ...

It might have been blue satin, Peter Stuyvesant Gold,
Deep Heat, umbrella pines, familiar two-note calls
repeated at intervals, a lifeguard's upraised hand.
It didn't matter what it was, almost anything would do
to bring it all back to you, then take it away again.

Day Return

Your thoughts race ahead of you down the line
to where the day is building
a strange new town for you to arrive in:
the ruined castle,
the different-coloured buses,
the girl from the office
who tears up your day return
and throws it in pieces at your feet.

You smile for no reason
at a cut-out of two workmen
carrying a ladder across a field
on behalf of 'KARPIN BROS REMOVALS AND
    DECORATIONS'.
Even the horses looking up from grass
seem to agree that time and you

are flying past for once
without knowing why exactly.

Sealink

On the boat, we foot passengers
were shuffled like a pack of cards
and thrown down in new combinations
all over the half-empty, off-season decks.
Children bumped into one another.
Parents looked for somewhere quiet to sit
away from the video games.
Young couples ate enormous, nervous meals,
while single people roamed back and forth
between the restaurant and Duty Free.

As land came into sight, one asked another
'Do you know the way back to the coach?
I think it's on Whale Deck.'
A conversation begins with 'May I sit
next to you? God, it's hot in here!
Do you mind if I open this window?'
We take off our coats, settle back, peel oranges.
Shall we speak in English or French?
Are we going on holiday? Or home?
Do we mind knowing each other's name?

Straw Dogs

When she says I have the gift of the gab
her dress is off the shoulder,
her breath is warm on my cheek. I talk so fast
about my brother's films and friends

I grow hoarse shouting their first names
over the Rolling Stones.
'STRAW DOGS' I yell to the room
as the music stops unexpectedly.

My Chances

As I grew warmer
and the bus went over the bumps,
I let my mind wander
further and further,
checking my scowl
in the window of the bus
against my chances
of bending her over that table,
the arm of that chair.

When she answered the door
in her low-cut dress
I forgot what it was
I was going to do to her.
I gave her a kiss
and asked if she was ready to go out,
checking my smile

in the mirror in the hall
against my chances of being liked.

Till Soon

How I laughed at your orders.
I shall obey them to the letter,
not forgetting the short-back-and-sides
and the shirt that isn't button-down.
I agree with you about the car.
Why suffer when we can travel in comfort?
Just let the weather be fine,
but it doesn't matter what it's like
so long as we can walk around together
and make fun of everything,
the way we did last time.

Interval

Scene shifters have come on
under cover of dark,
anonymous creatures
in soft shoes and black pullovers,
who move about the stage
with easy familiarity,
scattering magazines,
resetting the hands of a clock.

They change the position of a lamp
or piece of furniture,

butting it with a hip,
nudging it into the future.
A couple of cushions on the floor,
the angle of a sofa,
are all we need to know
about a missing hour.

During an Absence

Now that she has left the room for a moment
to powder her nose,
we watch and wait, watch and wait,
for her to bring back the purpose into our lives.

How

You fell asleep in your chair
and woke up some time later
and said, 'It's hot in here'
and asked for a glass of water.

How you stretched out your hand for the glass
and a look came into your eye
which might have been laziness
or might have been lechery.

Collarbone

Your hair hacked close to your head
by someone calling herself a friend,
the gap in your teeth, the squint,
the grown-up, own-up evening gown,
the delicate collarbone
you would one day fall and break.

The fracture was serious enough
to require two pins – a crooked line of stitches
where I had kissed you.
Only three days after the operation
you wanted to go to bed
and only cried out once.

Timer

The smell of ammonia in the entrance hall.
The racing bike. The junk mail.
The timer switch whose single naked bulb
allowed us as far as the first floor.
The backs of your legs
as you went ahead of me up the stairs.

The landing where we paused for breath
and impatient key searching.
The locks which would never open quickly enough
to let us in.
The green of the paintwork we slid down
as if we had nowhere else to go.

Nothing On

Alone at last
and plastered from the mini-bar
we were looking around
for something to amuse us
in the hotel room
when you fell upon
the Gideon Bible
in the bedside table
and made me read to you
from the Book of Genesis.

If you carry on
dancing round the room like that
in your sun-tan swim-suit
twirling the hotel's
complimentary fruitbowl
it won't be long
till the page fills up
with four-letter words
and I lose my place
in the story of the Creation.

Rhetorical Questions

How do you think I feel
when you make me talk to you
and won't let me stop
till the words turn into a moan?
Do you think I mind
when you put your hand over my mouth

and tell me not to move
so you can 'hear' it happening?

And how do you think I like it
when you tell me what to do
and your mouth opens
and you look straight through me?
Do you think I mind
when the blank expression comes
and you set off alone
down the hall of collapsing columns?

The Lisboa

Pass me the alarm clock, Carolyn.
What time do you have to go to work?
I'll set it for half past seven,
then we'll have time for breakfast.
I'll get the milk.

Listen, why don't you ring up in the morning
and say you're going to be late?
Then we can do what we like.
We could go to the Lisboa and have custard tarts.
We could go to the Gate.

Lift up your arms.
Let me take this off.

Our Theory

Though working out of
different locations
too much of the time
on one occasion at least
we arrived at
similar conclusions.

Your voice on the phone
had been outlining
a theory of displacement
hingeing on a single
practical experiment
you were performing.

I hung on the line
excitedly roughing out
my response to your ideas
all fingers and thumbs
as I let my thoughts pour out
on a blank sheet.

Billy's Rain

When I'm lying awake, listening to rain
hammering on the roof,
the phrase comes back to me,
our code for 'Let's get out of here'.
We were huddled in the back of a van
with the lights, the videotape equipment
and the man with the rain machine.

'Why can't we use the regular rain?' you asked,
as rain hammered on the roof.
'That's God's rain,' said someone.
'It doesn't show up on film.
We need Billy's rain for this one.'
When I find myself soaked to the skin, tired,
or merely bored with God's rain,
the phrase comes back to me.
I'd say it now if I thought you were listening.

Cross Country

The train drivels north in a series
of false starts and broken promises,
pauses for thought alongside a giant blonde.
Only another hour till I see you,
running down the platform to meet me,
I don't think I can wait that long.

Everywhere I look, little passionate scenes
are being played out against a background
of hurrying clouds. Every couple I see
fills me with insane jealousy.
What does she see in him?
What does he see in her?
Why is love between other people so tender and pure?

At Euston Station I found myself standing next to a man
with the same overnight bag as me,
looking at the same middle-aged woman
who smoothed her jumper over low-slung breasts.
I was so excited I got on the train before mine,

a sadistic 'Cross Country' affair
which dawdles between stations, making me beg for it.

Here's a woman I already feel close to
after only half an hour
of trying not to look at her bare arms.
She lifts them above her head
in a gesture of boredom or surrender.
Her hands touch in mid-air and she turns them
inside out in a kind of question mark.
I'm carrying my head on a platter.
If I make a move I'll probably spill myself.

Late

By the time we limp into Manchester
half an hour late, the moment has been lost
when I might have passed myself off
as myself. I wave as usual,

but you look straight through me,
searching other faces in the crowd
for someone you thought you would recognize
if you ever saw him again.

Lost Weekend

The hotel cost too much
so we didn't even touch the bed
and said we'd decided
not to take it after all

and just picked up our things
and set off down the road
till we came to this youth hostel
in an old hospital

and asked ourselves quietly
what we were doing there
and laid out the remains of the picnic
and took stock of the situation.

Get that chair over there
and we'll just sit here and talk.
It's been a long day. Our feet hurt.
Our money is running out.

When I've calmed down a bit
I'll go out and see if I can find such a thing
as a bottle of wine
in this godforsaken town.

Among the Combs

Among the combs and face creams
of her childhood sponge-bag,
tangled with her hair –
the green-and-silver blister pack
marked with the days of the week.

We follow the arrows printed on the pack
and move around clockwise.
The days fly past in an endless stream,
leaving only a rip in the tinfoil
and nothing in the world to fear.

At the Brief Encounter

Five minutes left to go in this pink-shot
station café, being stared at by a boy.
What shall we do? What shall we say?

I know. Let's cry. Let's scream.
Let's tear down the station with our bare hands.
Let's scatter it to the four winds.

Token

For I am sorry about what happened at the fairground
the other day.
For I regret not going on any of the rides.
For I am sending this token of my resolution to do
better next time, if there is a next time.
For I undertake to escort the holder on the Big Dipper,
the Golden Galloper, the Chair-O-Plane, the Wagon
Wheel and anything else she wants to go on.
For that includes the Whip, the Pirate Ship, the Surf
Dancer and the Wind Runner.
For I also promise to accompany her on the
Underwater Adventure.
For I further guarantee not to chicken out of the Crater.
For I am willing to enter the Haunted House, if she
will go in with me.
For I am even willing to go on the Bumping Cars,
which proves how much I love her.
For if all this fails to please her I will grow a pair of
wings for the occasion and fly with her across the sky.

Last Things

They must be checking our location on the map,
taking leave of their loved ones,
asking the way to our house.

They are not in any hurry to get here.
They have a certain schedule to stick to.
They know where we are.

If we try to see them, outlined against the horizon,
they stand completely still, looking innocent.
If we turn our backs on them, they move
forward again, more confident.

One evening, when nothing much is going on,
they detach themselves from the surrounding
    countryside
and begin their advance across no-man's-land.
They make themselves known to us
in a ripple of ill-wind.

Lunch Hour

On a traffic island
    buses sway the flowers
        people trot across

Some stay on the seat
    light a cigarette
        unfold their newspapers

Sun is out all day
shining on metal
we sit on the wall

Astonishing how similar
minute by minute
dream you are fine

All Right

I'm lying awake somewhere between
the yellow pilot-light
of the Dimplex thermostat
and the winking eye of the fax,
making the journey across town,
past all the stations in North London,
going over Bishop's Bridge,
entering the badlands.

I hear your giggles as I hit the bumps
in the curved section
of Westbourne Park Road.
I see the crack of light in your curtains
when I stop at the lights
at the corner of Ladbroke Grove.
If you go past your window now
everything will be all right.

Rainy Night

Something about the hiss of a taxi
cruising an empty street,
its foggy yellow light
skidding off piles of black bin-liners
is trying to let me know
this isn't my night.

Something about the look of your front door,
its familiar fanlight star
picked out in black
is trying to get through to me
that you and I
have turned some sort of corner.

Rain off the river, mixed with the smell
of pavements in summer,
is trying to let me down lightly.
I stand on the step
while the sound of your doorbell
echoes down the hall.

Their Holidays

Striped light coming through the blinds
and falling on the bed
where the man and woman are kneeling.

I don't know what they are doing.
I don't really care.
I said, 'Hello, what are you doing here?'

I was standing in the middle of the room
trying to make a telephone call.
I kept taking the receiver off the hook

and putting it back again.
I moved forward, to where I would remain,
standing at the foot of the bed.

It was something like a dog and bitch
who craned their necks around,
striped light coming through the blinds.

Dangerous Water

Don't go over there, Carolyn,
past the nightclub, past the boats, past the rocks,
where the waves come furthest up the beach
in natural swimming pools.

It's deserted over there now,
except for one or two fishermen and one or two couples
looking for a place to be alone.
I don't like to think of you over there.

I don't like to think of you
when the tide suddenly turns
and the sun goes down behind the town.
You could get cut off over there, as we should know.

And don't try to swim for it, the way you did last time.
Wait till I get there.
Then we'll have to spend the night together
in the old Rasta Bar.

Strange Meeting

I ring up in the usual way,
but something's not quite right.
Instead of saying 'Hello, how are you?
Can you come out to play?'
she suggests 'meeting up' some time,
which makes my blood run cold.
I'm on my way round there now
with flowers and other apologies.

For a moment the doorbell excites me
with scenes out of the past,
but the kiss on both cheeks
and the cheerful look on her face
as she takes my coat for me
are pointers to a brand new future
she ushers me into now
and asks me to sit down.

Nothing Stinted

We have taken up our positions
over a complicated board game
of coffee, cigarettes, wine
(nothing stinted for the occasion)
while she tells me with a certain sadness
how she's got 'muddled up' with her boss.

I come out of my corner laughing, likeable,
full of stories about my trip.
I refill her glass for her.

Feigning concern for her welfare
and knowing her openness on the subject,
I ask about birth control.
What method are they using?
Are they being careful?

She leans towards me across the table.
'Remember you used to tell me
men would always treat me badly if I let them?
Well, he doesn't. He treats me well.
You don't have to worry about that.'

Congratulations

It looks at first like a horse
failing repeatedly to clear a fence,
rearing up, stalling for a moment,
sinking down between her thighs.
I watch from my vantage point
as she urges him on with her heel.
Given that sort of encouragement,
and seeing the look on her face,
I feel sure I would make a better job
of surmounting such an obstacle,
but there's no getting away from the fact
that she finds his efforts acceptable,
even, now that he is sprawled all
over her, worthy of congratulation.

Unobtainable

Whether it was putting in an extra beat
or leaving one out, I couldn't tell.
My heart seemed to have forgotten
everything it ever knew
about timing and co-ordination
in its efforts to get through to someone
on the other side of a wall.
As I lay in bed, I could hear it
hammering away inside my pillow,
being answered now and then
by a distant guitar-note of bedsprings,
pausing for a moment, as if listening,
then hurrying on as before.

Alternator

To be in possession of the facts, yet powerless,
is new to me, a strange technology
of waiting, hanging by a thread,
watching the dud decisions
fizzing and popping in the night,
like this moth-crazed street light,
its opposite poles rigged to an alternator
of breaking up or asking her to marry me.

I make my heart beat, remembering her silences.
My brains fly out through the top of my head.
Run to the ends of the earth?
Or set up camp on her doorstep?
I take my place on her answering tape.

My innocent enquiries. My carefree messages.
'The phone was ringing when I came in ...
I was wondering if you'd got my letter ...'

Blindfold Games

It isn't so much that he loves her
and wants to marry her
that keeps me awake at night
as the thought of them stumbling upstairs together
in a sort of three-legged race.

I only have to close my eyes
and he is taking her by the arm,
pushing her towards the bedroom.
He has left the door half open,
but I can't quite see what they are doing,
only glimpses from time to time,
the backs of her legs, the scar on her shoulder.

I turn to look away,
but the shock of her pleasure rises in my throat,
the insult of her sweat mingling with his sweat,
her saying certain things,
her throwing out one arm.

Live Bed Show

For I notice it isn't me
bumping so realistically against her thighs,
leaning forward, whispering in her ear

unscripted obscenities.
For I remember playing the same part myself
in another lifetime.
For those were the days
when she and I never tired
of improvising fresh pieces of action.
For we thought and acted as one.

For I notice it isn't me
rising above her now, simulating climax.
For I have to admit
she enters into the spirit of the thing
with uncanny conviction.
For I keep reminding myself
that nothing is really happening between them.
For it seems so unlikely somehow.
For I must be imagining things.
For I take some comfort from this.

Sweet Nothings

Not her mouth not her chin not her throat.
Not her smell not her skin not her sweat.

No laughs and no jokes and no thoughts.
No words and no desires – none of that any more.

None of that any more and all of it still.
All of it still and more and more of it every day.

All That

And then there's the one you write
that makes even you laugh.
You never want to see her again.
You don't want to see her handwriting
on a letter. You don't want to come home
and see the little yellow light
flashing messages of regret.
You don't want to pick up the phone
and hear how much she's been missing you.
Couldn't you meet for a drink?
Not any more. Maybe in a year or two.
All you want to do now
is draw a line under your life
and get on with the past.
Do you make yourself perfectly clear?
You sign with just your name,
a businesslike touch
which makes even you laugh.

Haircut

How idiotic two months later
the hair curling over my collar
the fringe falling in my eyes
as I catch a glimpse in the mirror
of the haircut she arranged
the haircut she supervised
its stupidity its ignorance its bliss.

How I envy my last haircut
that knows nothing of all this
that cannot hear her voice
laughing and apologising
for the haircut by her friend
the haircut that would soon grow out
its innocence its happiness its peace.

Useless

I narrowed it down to this –
her voice on the phone,
its cheerful 'Hello, how are you?
Can you come out to play?'
I wrapped her choking laugh
in layers of indifference.
I couldn't get rid of her mouth.

I narrowed it down once more –
a look on her face,
one arm across my neck.
As a final test
I allowed her to speak my name.
That was no good at all.
That was worse than useless.

Erosion

The cricketer proves my theory
of erosion, landslide, wilderness.

He teetered on the brink
of a difficult decision,
before coming down firmly
on the dining-room floor.

I almost caught him –
or did I give him a little push?
At any rate, he slipped through my fingers,
somersaulted once or twice
and made his eloquent last point
from all over the place.

Mirror History

Round about here I become aware of your
existence for the first time, that you might even
be alive, in the sense that I am alive,
walking around having thoughts about everything,
but keeping a pleasant expression on your face.
I wonder why it never struck me before
that you might not be happy all the time.

When I think about lovemaking for instance
it occurs to me that you might not have been
faking it after all, that perhaps it was me
who was putting on an act for your benefit.
As if you couldn't read me like a book!
How strange to think there were two of us
doing those things and I never realized.

Re-reading what I have written up till now
I am conscious only of what is not being said,
the mirror history running underneath all this

self-pitying nonsense. To hear me talk
you'd think I was the aggrieved party,
whereas we both know it was my own decision
to do nothing that made nothing happen.

Even as we were breaking up for the last time
I was looking at my watch behind your back,
thinking: what shall we do next? Through my tears
I made out the hands telling me I was late
for something or other, so I cut short my visit
and went dashing off across London on the bike,
telling myself I could always go back if I wanted to.

If only they were waiting for us somewhere,
the nights we didn't use, the things we didn't do,
the bridge we didn't lean on in the moonlight,
watching the barges pass beneath our feet.
Instead, a faint glimmer appears on the horizon,
as if someone were signalling through mist.
A ghost with a yellow shopping bag
waves to a yellow raincoat
at the other end of a street.

Some R&B and Black Pop

I refused to say anything
when Charlie and Inez Foxx sang 'Mockingbird',
or Oscar Wills sang 'Flat Foot Sam'.
I remained silent throughout Elmore James's version
of 'Stormy Monday'. I didn't give in
to Gene Allison or Sonny Boy Williamson.

I broke down and admitted everything
when I reached the place on the tape
where Lazy Lester's 'I'm a Lover Not a Fighter'
suddenly gets much louder
and one of us always had to get out of bed
to turn the volume down.

Blank Pages

This is the room
where we struggled with the words to your songs,
disjointed, two-note things
which seemed to have no refrains,

or lay awake in the same bed,
hearing our verses crackling all night
in the waste-paper basket:
paper flesh, blood ink.

The deadline came round
like a vast tick of the clock.
The minute hand moved on with a little jerk.
We laid aside our work.

And then the blank pages
at the end of an old notebook,
left behind in a suitcase,
taking up too much room under the stairs.

I'm writing in it now –
disjointed scenes from our life,
its early promise, personal triumphs,
eventual loss of faith.

How I held the door for you,
in ignorance of love,
dragging you back again too late to save the day.
How I did the same thing twice.

It sounds like one of our songs –
the dry laughter of tearing paper,
the sensation of falling,
of falling through the tear.

Early Morning

Each dawn might be peacetime again –
white empty skies, the glow of battle
turned to ash-coloured light.

For a little while longer
opposing forces sleep.
The linings of curtains look like flags of surrender.

A cry of pleasure is followed by a baby's cry.
Without this truce each day
God knows where we would be.

Everyone Knows This

How am I feeling this morning?
Or is it too early to say?
I check by swallowing
to see if my throat's still sore.

I check by thinking
to see if my brain still hurts.

I'm walking along out of doors,
not feeling anything much,
when it suddenly comes to me:
I don't feel so bad any more.
I think to myself,
'I'll soon put a stop to that!'

Bar Italia

How beautiful it would be to wait for you again
in the usual place,
not looking at the door,
keeping a lookout in the long mirror,
knowing that if you are late
it will not be too late,
knowing that all I have to do
is wait a little longer
and you will be pushing through the other customers,
out of breath, apologetic.
Where have you been, for God's sake?
I was starting to worry.

How long did we say we would wait
if one of us was held up?
It's been so long and still no sign of you.
As time goes by, I search other faces in the bar,
rearranging their features
until they are monstrous versions of you,
their heads wobbling from side to side

like heads on sticks.
Your absence inches forward
until it is standing next to me.
Now it has taken the seat I was saving.
Now we are face to face in the long mirror.

Legend

X's darken the map of London
in the places we made love.
Footprints hurry back and forth
from Chelsea to Ladbroke Grove.

Winged hearts accompany our progress.
Flaming arrows signify intent.
Grappling hooks are loving glances.
Handcuffs are kindly meant.

Knives and forks are for dining out.
Wine glasses are for romancing.
Skeletons mark the Latin American clubs
where we used to go dancing.

Siren Song

I phone from time to time, to see if she's
changed the music on her answerphone.
'Tell me in two words,' goes the recording,
'what you were going to tell me in a thousand.'

I peer into that thought, like peering out
to sea at night, hearing the sound of waves
breaking on rocks, knowing she is there,
listening, waiting for me to speak.

Once in a while she'll pick up the phone
and her voice sings to me out of the past.
The hair on the back of my neck stands up
as I catch her smell for a second.

Her News

You paused for a moment and I heard you smoking
on the other end of the line.
I pictured your expression,
one eye screwed shut against the smoke
as you waited for my reaction.
I was waiting for it myself, a list of my own news
gone suddenly cold in my hand.
Supposing my wife found out, what would happen then?
Would I have to leave her and marry you now?

Perhaps it wouldn't be so bad,
starting again with someone new, finding a new place,
pretending the best was yet to come.
It might even be fun,
playing the family man, walking around in the park
full of righteous indignation.
But no, I couldn't go through all that again,
not without my own wife being there,
not without her getting cross about everything.

Perhaps she wouldn't mind about the baby,
then we could buy a house in the country
and all move in together.
That sounded like a better idea.
Now that I'd been caught at last, a wave of relief
swept over me. I was just considering
a shed in the garden with a radio and a day bed,
when I remembered I hadn't seen you for over a year.
'Congratulations,' I said. 'When's it due?'

Balcony Scene

The street light shorting on and off,
casting a balcony on my bedroom wall.
I seem to have wired it up
to my thoughts of you, your first-floor studio,
the ladder to your bed, car lights overhead.

I was climbing the ladder one night
when I caught the eye of a man
going past on the top of a bus
and for one moment became him
as he turned to look back at us.
I fell asleep after that, never dreaming
I would give it a second thought.

I see his face now, passing my window,
as I draw the curtains for the night,
the street light shorting on and off,
somehow refusing to blow.

Index of First Lines

Index of Titles